Shipwreck of the *Mesquite*
Death of a United States Coast Guard Cutter

Frederick Stonehouse

Lake Superior Port Cities Inc.

First Edition: August 1991

5 4 3 2 1

LAKE SUPERIOR PORT CITIES INC.
P.O. Box 16417
Duluth, Minnesota 55816-0417
USA

DESIGN: Lynn Lynas
ILLUSTRATOR: Wesley Mutch
EDITOR: Paul L. Hayden
EDITORIAL SUPPORT: Tracy Claseman
TYPOGRAPHY: Stacy L. Winter
PRINTING: Davidson Printing Co.

Library of Congress Cataloging-In-Publication Data
Stonehouse, Frederick
  Shipwreck of the Mesquite
  Bibliography, p. 98.
    1. Shipwrecks — Superior, Lake. 2. Shipwrecks — Great Lakes. 3. Shipwrecks.
4. Lake Superior. 5. Mesquite (ship). 6. U.S. Coast Guard. 7. Salvage. 8. Skin Diving.
I. Title.

Library of Congress Card Catalog Number: 91-062082

ISBN 0-942235-10-x

Printed in the United States of America

FOREWORD

As an organization, the U.S. Coast Guard is spread very thin. There are roughly only 40,000 members to cover both coasts, from the middle of the Atlantic to the middle of the Pacific, Arctic to Antarctic, all U.S. navigable rivers and the Great Lakes.

In peacetime the Coast Guard is part of the Department of Transportation. In wartime, it transfers under the Navy. An old Coast Guard saying is that "the Coast Guard is that organization around which the Navy forms in time of war." Another one claims that the Navy spends 90 percent of its time training and 10 percent working. By contrast, the Coast Guard spends 10 percent of its time training and 90 percent of its time working.

The point is that the Coast Guard has tough and difficult jobs. Major missions include search and rescue, law enforcement, investigation of maritime accidents, pollution control, ice breaking and aids to navigation activities. It accomplishes these well and with minimal resources.

Although the *Mesquite* was technically a buoy tender, I often call her a cutter. The term is an old one in the Coast Guard, referring to the original sailing cutters that helped enforce the nation's early revenue laws. The term is applied by the Coast Guard to all vessels more than 65 feet in length.

To some degree the Coast Guard is a victim of its own success. As the old military saying goes, they have "done so much with so little for so long, they can now do anything with nothing." The Coast Guard seems to receive more missions with fewer resources. Surprisingly, it also seems to accomplish them! Consider, however, the fragile position the Coast Guard on the Great Lakes is in now as the result of the *Mesquite* loss and the lack of a replacement vessel.

Tending buoys is an important part of the Coast Guard's job.

It is grubby, cold work completely without glory of any sort — only the pride of a task well done. It calls for long, hard hours and, based on the nature of the work, is certainly high-stress.

Maintaining the aids on the Great Lakes depends largely on the 180-foot tenders like the *Mesquite*. They are not flashy or fast. Built during the height of World War II, they are rapidly approaching old age. But they do carry themselves well, with a certain air of purposefulness and a pride in the work they do so well.

In the old days of lake navigation, Keweenaw Point was notorious among sailors. Often it was called the most dangerous point on the lakes. An estimated 51 vessels were wrecked in the vicinity! While many improvements, notably radar, have largely eliminated it as a major hazard, it still waits for the unwary as evidenced by the *Mesquite*.

The Keweenaw Point buoy marks the easternmost shoal, important especially for vessels seeking shelter from a northerly or northwesterly gale. The buoy is critical not in terms of the vessels that wrecked in the vicinity, but rather for the ones that didn't. After all, that is the true purpose of aids to navigation, to avoid danger.

With the exception of identifying those members of the crew of the *Mesquite* who were either disciplined or honored for their part in the accident, I have mentioned no other crew member by name. This was purposely done. While being a member of the crew of a vessel lost due to "error" is not necessarily a dishonor, neither is it an honor. It is perhaps best forgotten.

I have also chosen to use the full titles of the principal players rather than more common terms or military abbreviations. Thus Commanding Officer is used instead of the more vernacular CO, Officer of the Deck instead of OOD and Engineering Officer instead of EO. The exception is when a direct quote is used. I have also used the full military spelling of rank in lieu of the military abbreviation: Lieutenant Commander instead of Lt. Cmdr. and Chief Warrant Officer instead of CWO.

Frederick Stonehouse
July 1991

ACKNOWLEDGMENTS

Completing a text of this nature requires the help of numerous individuals and institutions. I should particularly like to thank the following:

Public Affairs Office, Atlantic Area, United States Coast Guard

Public Affairs Office, Ninth Coast District, United States Coast Guard

Steve Abraitis

Captain Jimmie Hobaugh

Pat Labadie, Canal Park Marine Museum

William Meierhoff

Mark Rowe

Eric Smith

CONTENTS

PREFACE

Her mission wasn't the most glamorous in the world, but it was important and for 40-odd years she had done it well. From the time the naval architect first took pencil to paper, it was a task she had been designed specifically for: to maintain buoys, or aids to navigation as they are called today.

But this time it would be different. This time would be her last. Lake Superior would claim another.

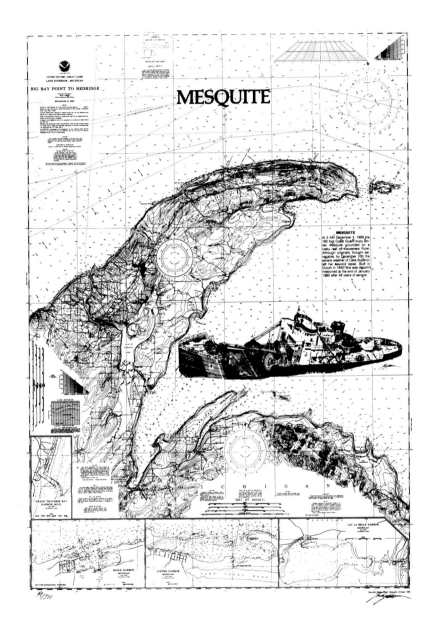

MESQUITE

UNITED STATES - GREAT LAKES
LAKE SUPERIOR - MICHIGAN

BIG BAY POINT TO REDRIDGE

MESQUITE

At 2 AM December 4, 1989 the 180 foot Coast Guard buoy tender Mesquite grounded on a rocky reef off Keweenaw Point. Although originally thought salvagable, by December 10th the severe weather of Lake Superior left her beyond repair. Built in Duluth in 1942, she was decommissioned at the end of January 1990 after 48 years of service.

GRAND TRAVERSE BAY
HARBOR, MICH.

EAGLE HARBOR
MICHIGAN

COPPER HARBOR
MICHIGAN

LAC LA BELLE HARBOR
MICHIGAN

The *Mesquite* rests on the rocks at Keweenaw Point, Michigan. Early Winter 1989-90.

Chapter 1

THE NEWS HITS

Coast Guard Cutter Lost
Off Keweenaw Point

At 2 a.m. on the morning of Monday, December 4, 1989, the 180-foot Coast Guard buoy tender *Mesquite* ran aground in 12 feet of the dark, icy waters of Lake Superior off Keweenaw Point in Michigan's Upper Peninsula. With a crew of 53 aboard, the cutter was in the process of removing aids to navigation from the lake prior to winter freeze.

The *Mesquite* suffered severe damage which caused extensive flooding of the engine room. A list to the port side developed, and by 6:20 a.m. Lt. Cmdr. J.R. Lynch, the commanding officer, had ordered abandon ship. Three of the crew of the *Mesquite* were injured and were medivaced to the hospital at Hancock, Michigan, from the commercial vessel *Mangal Desai*, which came to their aid during the process.

Initial concerns were for the welfare of the crew and containment of any fuel leakage into the lake. In the days following the grounding, a containment boom was put into place around the cutter. Approximately 19,000 gallons of diesel fuel were then pumped off the cutter. Other valuable equipment aboard the vessel was also removed.

Severe weather following the accident left the ship in a poor

1

condition. Ten-foot seas and 30-knot winds over the next week-end broke the mast and enlarged holes in the hull. A team of divers inspected the condition of the hull and found holes as large as two feet in diameter and the rudder broken off. Within days whole sections of the hull dropped off into the lake.

By mid-December, the Coast Guard had determined that the cutter could not be saved. The vessel was considered a "constructive total loss." Historians considered this the worst vessel accident to occur on Lake Superior since the grounding of the *Frontenac* at Silver Bay, Minnesota, in November 1979. It was also the most costly government vessel loss in the history of Lake Superior. The vessel cost approximately $894,000 to build. It would cost $44 million to replace her. Although some of the buoys on board the cutter were removed, the Coast Guard would wait until spring to determine the disposition of the ship.

Paul Halvorson, one of the pilots of the *Mangal Desai* who rescued the cutter's crew, was awarded a U.S. Coast Guard commendation for his heroic efforts.

The *Mesquite* was built in 1942 by Marine Iron and Ship Building Company of Duluth, Minnesota. Her home base was Charlevoix, Michigan. Four other U.S. buoy tenders still operate on the Great Lakes: the *Bramble, Sundew, Acacia* and *Mariposa.*

Summary Report by *Lake Superior Magazine,* February 1990

Storm damage is evident on December 9, 1989, five days after the *Mesquite*'s grounding off Keweenaw Point.

Chapter 2

THE CUTTERS

The *Mesquite*'s keel was laid on August 20, 1942. Launched on November 14, 1942, she was commissioned on August 27, 1943. The total cost was $894,000. The contractor was Marine Iron & Ship Building Company of Duluth, Minnesota. She displaced 1,028 tons full and had a length overall of 180 feet, beam of 37 feet and draft of 14 feet. The power plant consisted of one electric motor connected to two Westinghouse generators driven by two Cooper-Bessemer diesels. Shaft horsepower was 1,200. Having a single screw, her maximum speed was 13 knots and nine knots economy. Cruising range was in excess of 30,000 miles. She was equipped with a 20-ton boom.

The original design work on the 180-foot class of buoy tenders was done by the old U.S. Light House Service before it amalgamated into the Coast Guard. The Coast Guard modified the plans to provide a more capable vessel.

The Light House Service designed their vessels as pure tenders and for service in a specific area. There were no true "classes" of vessels. Characteristics critical to the Light House Service were shallow draft to ease work near reefs and shoals, and twin screws for maneuverability. By contrast, the Coast Guard wanted vessels that were multi-mission — able to perform the duties of cutters as well as tenders.

The Coast Guard changed the original 180-foot design to

Top: In 1943, the Marine Iron & Ship Building construction yard at Duluth, Minnesota, was busy on five Coast Guard cutters. *Bottom:* Workers assemble a section for one of the cutters at Marine Iron.

draw 13 feet, four feet more than the newest Light House Service tender, the 177-foot *Juniper* built in 1939. In addition, they sacrificed twin-screw maneuverability for the increased immunity from ice damage of the single screw. The tenders were also strengthened to provide some ice breaking capability.

A total of 39 180-foot tenders were constructed. They were built in three sets, the first consisting of the *Cactus, Balsam, Cowslip, Woodbine, Gentian, Laurel, Clover, Evergreen, Sorrel, Citrus, Conifer, Madrona* and *Tupelo*. The second set consisted of *Ironwood, Buttonwood, Planetree, Papaw, Sweetgum* and *Mesquite*. With the exception of the *Ironwood*, which was built by the Coast Guard Yard at Curtis Bay, Maryland, all of the second set were built by Marine Iron & Ship Building in Duluth. The third set included *Basswood, Bittersweet, Blackhaw, Blackthorn, Bramble, Firebush, Hornbeam, Iris, Mallow,*

"M" - #76   M-W

MESQUITE: WORK IN PROGRESS: $695,000.00

#	MONTH: Year	PER CENT OF TOTAL	MATERIAL	LABOR	MATERIAL & LABOR	OVERHEAD	TOTAL	#
1	August 1942	01689	322347	643609	966056	208460	1174516	1
2	September "	09214	24876 05	30 44559	55121 64	8913 14	6403478	2
3	October "	18753	48 459 64	643 18 09	1123726 64	1795941	130332 15	3
4	November "	22965	570 4727	799137 0	13700047	2260596	15360746	4
5	December "	25714	63 340 63	80 84851	15718914	2755760	17874874	5
6	January 1943	28293	7373081	9322768	16655847	2967461	19662310	6
7	February 1943	34637	102349 65	162287 41	264577694	3615871	36037257	7
8	March - "	39772	117 81300	118088 66	2360 0166	4111439	27644605	8
9	April - "	48139	143 12191	141 18756	28430947	5025588	33456535	9
10	May - "	60161	17901528	1718638	3560831 66	6723948	41812114	10
11	June - "	78117	21771820	20488900	42260120	8556330	50816500	11
12	July - "	84329	25968336	22963490	4889 18 76	9716572	58608448	12
13	August - "	89982	2758872 1	24449760	52080621	10456992	62536113	13
14	September - "	93252	29606628	24571 166	5417794 64	10632031	64809825	14
15	October - "	93918	30032896	24608314	5464 1816	10632031	65273241	15
16	November - "	94184	30202706	24632752	54825488	10632031	65457519	16
17	December - "	94340	30300854	24633750	54934604	10632031	65566435	17
18	January - 1944	94091	30119018	24642878	54761296	10632031	65393327	18
19	February - "	94483	30387316	25037176	55037176	10632031	65697207	19
20	April - "	94287	30249016	24648160	5489 18 76	10632031	65529207	20
21	July - "	94266	30235016	24648160	54883176	10632031	65515207	21
22								22
23								23
24								24

Marine Iron bookkeepers kept a detailed account of the *Mesquite*'s construction costs.

5

In early 1943, five of the six *Mesquite* class cutters had been launched by Marine Iron & Ship Building in Duluth.

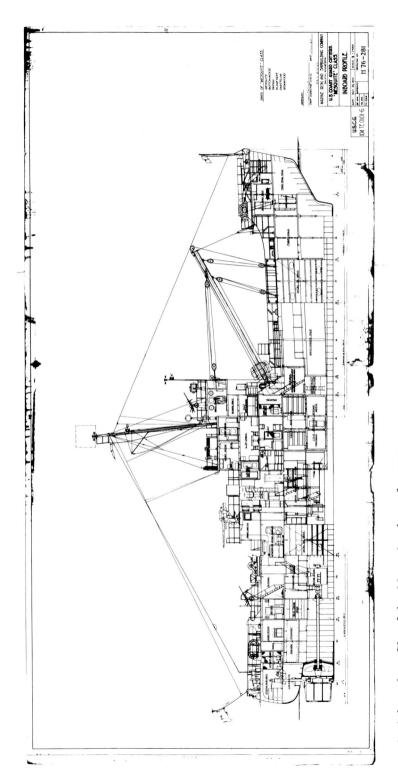

An inboard profile of the *Mesquite* class of cutters.

Top: Workers outfitted the cutters after they were afloat at Marine Iron.
Bottom: The launch of one of the Coast Guard cutters in Duluth.

Mariposa, Redbud, Sagebrush, Salvia, Sassafras, Sedge, Spar, Sundew, Sweetbriar, Acacia and *Woodrush*. Although all were the same class, there were some differences between them in the areas of cost, shaft horsepower and speed. Twenty-seven are still in service.

The 180s were often referred to as *Cactus* class tenders, since that was the lead vessel of the first set. The last tender built of the three sets was *Woodrush*. She is still in service on the lakes, as are *Acacia, Bramble* and *Sundew*. All 39 were World War II construction and all of the vessels, with the exception of *Ironwood*, were built in Duluth either by the Zenith Dredge Company or Marine Iron & Ship Building. Since they were built during wartime, each originally carried a three-inch gun plus 20mm machine guns, as well as depth charge racks and projectors.

The ability of the Coast Guard to have the tenders built when the country's shipyards were overwhelmed with critical Navy construction was proof of the high regard in which these little tenders were held. Their jobs, although not glamorous, were vital to the Navy.

One of the first set, the *Balsam*, distinguished herself in a way other than tending buoys. Operating in the Pacific Theater, she sighted a Japanese submarine and, using her depth charge projectors, sank it! It was a remarkable feat of arms for a tender.

The *Mesquite* also served in the Pacific. From 1944 until the end of the war, she sailed with the Seventh Fleet, including a period of duty in the Philippines.

The *Woodrush* had a special brush with fame. She was the first Coast Guard vessel to reach the scene of the *Edmund Fitzgerald* disaster on November 11, 1975. The tender sailed through the middle of a gale-whipped lake to reach it, to no avail.

The *Mesquite*'s life after the war was full of duties typical to a buoy tender: servicing aids to navigation, breaking spring ice and occasionally aiding vessels in trouble. In March 1985, during a law enforcement cruise in the Caribbean, she seized the Cayman M/V *Cruz Del Sur* with three pounds of marijuana. From September 1, 1947, through September 15, 1959, she was stationed at Sault Ste. Marie, Michigan. September 16, 1959,

The *Acacia* sat in dry dock while final installations were made.

through 1977 she was home ported at Sturgeon Bay, Wisconsin, and from 1977 until her loss at Charlevoix, Michigan.

In the mid- to late-1970s, the *Mesquite*, along with 13 other 180s, including the *Bramble, Sundew, Acacia* and *Woodrush*, underwent major renovations. At one point all of these cutters were scheduled for replacement in the mid-1990s.

Chapter 3

THE GROUNDING

A nytime a major vessel is lost, especially a government one, there is a fair amount of confusion, embarrassment and finger-pointing as to the exact cause. The facts may be plain enough, but sometimes they do not tell the whole story. Afterwards there can be as many versions — all true — as there were witnesses. Such a plethora of information can overload any attempt to piece together the truth.

The information in this chapter is drawn directly from the official U.S. Coast Guard reports of investigation. There is no reason to dispute any of the data.

As directed by the Commander, Ninth Coast Guard District and in accordance with the Coast Guard Administrative Investigations Manual, a single-officer Informal Board of Investigation was convened to "investigate the facts and circumstances surrounding the grounding of the U.S.C.G.C. *Mesquite* (WLB-305)." Captain Robert J. Parsons, the Commanding Officer of the icebreaker *Mackinaw*, was detailed to this duty.

The investigation was completed in accordance with Article 31, (b) Uniform Code of Military Justice. This important article prohibits compulsory self-incrimination and establishes the right to consult with an attorney. Service members must understand their rights before answering questions.

Following the accident, drug tests were routinely conducted

of key leadership personnel. All were negative.

Every person aboard at the time of grounding was interviewed. All documentary materials, including ship's logs, charts, records and instructions, were examined. The final copy of the informal report was provided to the Coast Guard's formal board on January 10, 1990.

The formal board met at the Coast Guard air station at Traverse City, Michigan, on December 10, 1989, and received a brief from the informal board concerning preliminary results. The board transferred to Charlevoix on December 11 as a more convenient location for witnesses. Testimony was taken for seven days from 23 witnesses and parties. On December 19 the board recessed with the record open. The formal report was completed on April 1, 1990.

The formal report was reviewed by the Commander, United States Coast Guard, Atlantic Region. His actions were released on June 26, 1990.

To give the reader an appreciation of the investigation process, I have included edited portions of both reports and the con-

The U.S. Coast Guard cutter *Mesquite* during good times.

The cutter *Sundew* was in for repairs, necessitating the *Mesquite*'s presence in Lake Superior to retrieve buoys for the winter.

vening authority actions. In some instances, there are significant differences, especially concerning evaluations of crew proficiency. What does become apparent through all the documents is the clear and precise investigative approach, the requirements for evidence of actions and the concern for possible corrective recommendations.

The *Mesquite* left her home port of Charlevoix, Michigan, on November 9, 1990, to start the winter buoy run. It is normal practice in the Ninth District for buoy tenders to decommission certain buoys in the winter and replace them in the spring.

The cutter had worked on various buoys in its normal area of operations in Lake Michigan from Chicago, Illinois, around the Straits of Mackinaw and to Cheboygan, Michigan, on Lake Huron. She was not out constantly, but rather returned to Charlevoix several times.

The *Mesquite* was sent north to work the Lake Superior buoys because *Sundew*, the usual Lake Superior tender, was in dry dock in Sturgeon Bay, Wisconsin. *Sundew* was home ported at

Duluth, Minnesota. On the evening of November 26, the *Mesquite* locked through Sault Ste. Marie, Michigan, to begin *Sundew*'s buoy duties.

Fifty-three personnel were aboard the cutter, including three from the National Data Buoy Office. They were to assist with the decommissioning of several National Oceanic and Atmospheric Administration (NOAA) buoys. In addition, there were one officer and two enlisted crew members from the *Sundew* to provide local knowledge and supplement the crew.

Late evening of December 1, 1989, found the *Mesquite* safely anchored in Schreiber Channel, Ontario, on the north side of Lake Superior. High winds and seas prevented her from decommissioning a Canadian weather buoy near the Slate Islands. The *Mesquite* was working the Canadian buoy because the Canadian Coast Guard was on strike and no one else was available to accomplish the job. The rough weather continued into December. To allow the crew to catch up on much-needed rest and relaxation, they were granted holiday leave. Once a break in the weather came, the crew would have to work hard to catch up.

Early on the 3rd the seas calmed sufficiently, so at 0814 hours the *Mesquite* hauled anchor and headed for the Canadian buoy.

Since Canadian Coast Guard crews were on strike, the *Mesquite* took over the buoy retrieving duties of the *Samuel Risley*.

14

The *Mesquite* was based in Charlevoix, Michigan. The ship's last voyage took her through the locks at Sault Ste. Marie and onto Lake Superior, where she retrieved several weather buoys before ending up on the rocks at Keweenaw Point in Michigan's Upper Peninsula.

At about 1000 hours she reached the buoy and decommissioned it. She then set course for the second buoy, the easternmost NOAA buoy in Lake Superior. She reached it at approximately 1900 hours. As is normal for the lateness of the season, the NOAA buoys were heavily coated with ice. Between 10 and 30 minutes were spent removing it from each buoy.

With the NOAA missions completed, the *Mesquite* headed for the Keweenaw Point buoy. When it was finished, she would proceed to the Keweenaw Waterway and three more buoys. Then her Lake Superior duty would be over. Between November 9 and December 3, she had worked 26 buoys.

When the *Mesquite* reached the Keweenaw Point area at 0100 hours on December 4, the weather was poor but far from bad. The wind was 190 degrees true (slightly west of south) at 16 knots. Visibility was 10 miles, the sky completely overcast and the temperature a chilly 23 degrees F. The seas ran one to two feet from 190 degrees true and the swell two to three feet at 200 degrees true.

At 0047 hours buoy handling stations were set in preparation for recovering the buoy. In accordance with the Commanding Officer's Night Orders for the 3rd, this consisted only of necessary personnel for deck and bridge operations. Besides the Officer of the Deck (OOD), this included two quartermasters for the buoy positioning team, a radar operator, the watchman (used for buoy operations) and the Quartermaster of the Watch. No lookout was posted. Regular buoy handling stations were not set because of the late hour.

About a half hour before approaching the buoy, Lieutenant Commander J. Richard Lynch, the Commanding Officer, came on the bridge and assessed the situation. At 34 years of age, Lynch had been in command of the *Mesquite* for five months. He was a 12-year Coast Guard veteran and had four and one-half years of sea duty. The *Mesquite* was his first command.

Ensign Susan L. Subocz was the Officer of the Deck and Conning Officer. A Conning Officer is the officer in charge of the vessel during any particular watch. The Officer of the Deck acts on behalf of the Commanding Officer and is in temporary command of the vessel. Subocz had reported aboard the *Mesquite* the previous June, having just graduated from the Coast Guard Academy. She was fully qualified as an in-port and under-way Officer of the Deck. Her qualification letter as an Officer of the Deck for "all waters and for daytime and nighttime navigating" was only a week old, dated November 26, 1989. Although she had gone through her qualifications more quickly than usual, both the Commanding Officer and Executive Officer were confident in her ability.

As the cutter approached the point, the Commanding Officer stood on the starboard wing while Subocz, as the Conning

Coast Guard buoy tenders gathered in Duluth, Minnesota, for a rendezvous in 1989. Pictured are (left to right, foreground) *Mesquite, Mariposa,* (background) *Sundew* and *Acacia.*

The last voyage out of Duluth for the *Mesquite*, August 1989.

Officer, was at his right at the controls. The wing controls included both engine and bow thruster. Rudder commands had to be passed to the wheelsman on the bridge. Throughout the operation Subocz retained the duties of both the Officer of the Deck and Conning Officer and handled the maneuvering of the vessel. Although the Commanding Officer was present, it was the Conning Officer who was in charge.

The *Mesquite* had never worked the Keweenaw Point buoy before with any of her present crew. The officer from the *Sundew* did not suggest any special concerns or potential dangers.

Both engines and the bow thruster were on line and functioning properly. No steering problems were noted. All electronic

The *Mesquite*'s maneuvering controls on the starboard wing, like on this vessel, were used during buoy retrieving operations.

equipment was logged as operational without defects.

While approaching the buoy it was noted that the Gull Rock Light was extinguished. This meant that there was no visible object for a danger bearing. Instead, radar ranges were used from Keweenaw Point (400 yards) and Keystone Point (2.2 nautical miles) to navigate. The buoy positioning team had planned to use a danger range from both Keweenaw Point and Gull Rock.

A danger bearing is a line established so that a position on one side will assure the vessel of being in safe water, while a position on the other indicates a hazardous situation. A danger range is the minimum distance a vessel must stay beyond. To go closer places the vessel in danger.

Normal practice was for the navigator to "review and approve all track lines, danger bearings and ranges" as used for buoy handling operations. This was not done for the danger range.

The Global Positioning System (GPS) and Long Range Navigation (LORAN) were available and logged operational, but were not considered precise enough for accurate positioning.

The *Mesquite* approached the Keweenaw Point buoy into the wind, in order to work it on her starboard side. Throughout the process the cutter's bow would occasionally fall off to starboard.

The bridge of a 180-foot *Mesquite* class Coast Guard cutter.

The Conning Officer would bring it back using the bow thruster and coming ahead. The light was out and the buoy was first located on radar, then illuminated with the spotlight. It was found 55 yards, 070 degrees out of position and approximately 700 yards off Keweenaw Point. Water depth was 48 feet as measured with a lead line.

The particular buoy at Keweenaw Point was known as a 6 x 20, designed and constructed for semi-exposed or protected locations. 6 x 20 refers to six feet in diameter and 20 feet in length. The weight was 6,023 pounds. The nominal range of the daymark was 2.1 nautical miles and the radar range 2.4 nautical miles.

At 0110 hours on the 4th, the buoy was hooked and hauled on deck. When the sinker was at the water's edge, the *Mesquite* came to a heading of 270 degrees true and the Commanding Officer ordered the Conning Officer to back out to a distance of 1,000 yards off Keweenaw Point. The sinker is a large block of concrete weighing from 5,000 to 6,000 pounds that is used to hold the buoy in position.

After the *Mesquite* moved 890 yards off the point, she swung her bow back into the wind, a heading of approximately 190 degrees true. This was accomplished using the bow thruster and short bursts of left full rudder. When the maneuvering was finished, she had moved back towards Keweenaw Point and was 640 yards off. The sinker was now brought on deck. Their job apparently done, the radar operator and buoy positioning team left the bridge.

Neither the Commanding Officer nor the Officer of the Deck considered that the wind and current would have any appreciable effect on the *Mesquite* during the time she was off the Keweenaw. The National Search and Rescue Manual contained a graph that indicated that the leeway for a similar vessel in a 16-knot wind is about .65 knots, a significant amount.

The first navigational fix after the buoy was aboard was taken at 0208 hours by the Quartermaster of the Watch. It showed the vessel to be .225 nautical miles off Keweenaw Point, 2.42 nautical miles off Keystone Point and 3.60 nautical miles off Mani-

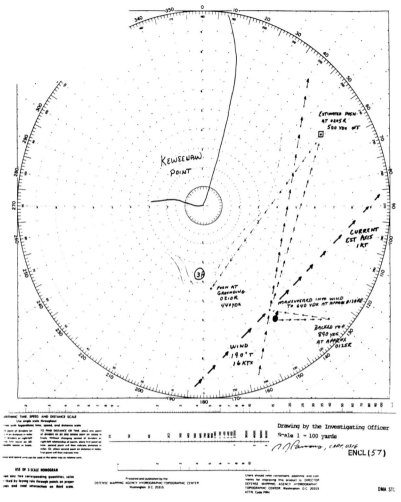

During the hearings into the grounding of the *Mesquite,* the investigating officer plotted the conjectured movements of the vessel on this imaging chart.

tou Island. No sounding was taken. From this position the Officer of the Deck thought she was north and east of the buoy position. The Officer of the Deck also verified the course away from the buoy site as 217 degrees true. Contrary to normal procedure, the Navigating Officer did not verify the track line run from the charted position of the buoy. The Officer of the Deck had no knowledge of a current in the area nor did the buoy file indicate one.

The Commanding Officer's written Standing Orders required the Officer of the Deck to:

- "When in pilot waters...determine the position at least every 15 minutes." And, "take a minimum of three LOPS (Lines Of Position Sight) for each fix whenever possible."
- "Obtain a sounding whenever a fix is obtained and check it against the charted depth."
- "...when operating in restricted waters, increase the frequency of your fixes."
- "...that the OOD maintain an alert lookout and to station a lookout."

The *Mesquite*'s Standing Orders were acknowledged in writing by Ensign Subocz on July 1, 1989, and by the Quartermaster of the Watch on December 2, 1989. These Standing Orders were promulgated in 1986 by the previous Commanding Officer and were not changed by Lieutenant Commander Lynch.

Coast Guard Regulations require the following:

- "Require that position of the vessel be known at all times in so far as it is feasible to do so by the utilization of navigational methods, devices and equipment in accordance with the highest standards of navigation and seamanship."
- "The OOD shall keep informed of the position of the ship and of all particulars which may be of use in keeping the ship out of danger, and shall employ such means and devices as may be available for directing and avoiding danger from grounding or collision."
- "The OOD shall station lookouts as circumstances require."

At 0200 hours the *Mesquite* was heading 226 degrees true with the speed various as the vessel got under way. Five minutes later the speed was 3.8 knots (60 turns) and the course 217 degrees true. With the deck load secured, the buoy working lights were turned off and buoy handling stations ended. Speed was increased to 120 turns. Full speed was 180 turns. It was planned that the cutter would be off the Upper Entry at first light. The Commanding Officer now left the bridge. He did not verify the position of the cutter before leaving. In the short interval the *Mesquite* spent working the buoy, the fickle Lake Superior weather had not changed.

At 0210 hours the *Mesquite* ran hard aground. Only the Officer of the Deck, quartermaster and one other crew member were on the bridge. Radar ranges showed her .250 nautical miles off Keweenaw Point, 2.19 nautical miles off Keystone Point and 3.78 nautical miles off Manitou Island. The three-foot shoal was clearly visible 60 to 70 yards away off the starboard bow.

Immediately upon striking, the Officer of the Deck backed the engines full and then brought them to all stop. The Commanding Officer, who had been on the mess deck, reached the bridge within one minute. When he asked the Officer of the Deck what happened, she replied, "I don't know. I think we ran aground."

The Commanding Officer immediately ordered General Quarters. The vessel was already rolling substantially from side to side and pounding on the shoal despite the calm weather.

The General Quarters alarm brought the Executive Officer to the bridge. He relieved Ensign Subocz of the deck and conn. The Operations Officer and Quartermaster of the Watch worked quickly to determine the best direction to try to back the vessel off. A quick check of the radar showed her to be 485 yards off Keweenaw Point.

At 0219 hours Station Duluth called the *Mesquite* to get a routine position report. In response, Ensign Subocz stated they were aground off Keweenaw Point and were assessing the situation. In turn Station Duluth notified the Ninth District Operations Center and Group Sault.

The Engineering Officer, Chief Warrant Officer Three (CWO3) James M. Thanasiu, was in the wardroom when the vessel struck. He was also in charge of Damage Control Central (DCC), a critical position if the *Mesquite* were to be saved. Damage Control Central was located in the *Mesquite*'s wardroom. As damage was discovered in other areas of the vessel, it was reported by sound powered phone to the DCC where it would be evaluated and corrective measures initiated. As the officer in charge, it was Thanasiu's responsibility to assess the damage and advise the Commanding Officer of what actions were necessary to counter it. Thanasiu was a 23-year Coast Guard veteran.

Based on his initial assessment, the Engineering Officer asked the Commanding Officer for permission to off-load the deck load and pump the forward peak tank. He also recommended that no attempt to back off be made until he could make a complete damage assessment. The *Mesquite* was now pounding four to six times a minute. On occasion it was severe enough to drive members of the crew to their knees!

Apparently the Commanding Officer and Engineering Officer never discussed or developed a salvage plan. The Commanding Officer was aware of the use of counter-flooding to stabilize a vessel, but did not consider it as an option for the *Mesquite*. Counter-flooding could have been used to help lessen or stop the *Mesquite*'s pounding on the bottom.

At 0237 hours the crew began to off-load the deck load, consisting of a 6 x 20 buoy, 5,000-pound and 6,500-pound sinkers, one shot of one-inch chain and 45 feet of one-and-one-eighth-

The RHI *Mes 2* inflatable raft on the *Mesquite* was identical to this one on another cutter. Note the twin outboard engines.

inch chain. Four NOAA buoys were to be left aboard.

Water was reported entering from the magazine space into dry stores. Although the leak was plugged and shored, the pounding caused the framework to flex. The compartment was abandoned and secured. A 10- to 12-inch crease was also discovered in the motor room.

At 0231 hours the Engineering Officer directed two of the crew to break out the survival suits and place them on deck for ready use. Also known as Gumby suits, the neoprene rubber suits would allow the crew to survive in the cold water. The Engineering Officer also had both small boats (*Mes 1* and *Mes 2*) readied in case the bridge requested them. *Mes 2* was a Rigid Hull Inflatable (RHI), and *Mes 1* was a Motor Cargo Boat (MCB). The RHI was a 20-foot Avon, powered by twin outboards and capable of carrying 15 personnel. The MCB was a 26-foot fiberglass work boat.

At 0240 hours the Engineering Officer advised the Commanding Officer that it was a good time to try, and the *Mesquite* attempted to back off using 100 turns. Five minutes later another attempt was made at 150 turns. The Damage Control Central advised the bridge to halt when the engines were ''vibrating widely on their mounts.'' The Commanding Officer had asked to use the bow thruster, but the Engineering Officer advised against it. The vessel had not moved.

Soundings were taken around the vessel at 0251 hours. The depth off the stern was 17 feet, at the starboard side aft portion of the forecastle 13 feet and forward about 12 feet. By now seas had increased to four feet.

At 0302 hours the *Mesquite* reported to Station Duluth that she had flooding in dry stores, engine room and magazine space, and that frame 92 in the engine room was buckling. Shortly thereafter the bridge reported that, ''We are holding our own.'' Flooding was estimated at three gallons per minute. The deck in the after berthing was also buckling. Several officers and crew helped bring emergency repair equipment to the site, but when they were half finished shoring it up, the first call to abandon ship was passed.

After the report of the grounding reached Coast Guard headquarters, the cutter *Katmai Bay* was dispatched from Group Sault to assist, although it was many hours before the ship would arrive.

To correct a four-degree port list, the Engineering Officer directed that the *Mes 2* (port boat) be lowered. The first attempt failed when the whip would not pay out because of ice. After a hasty repair, the boat was lowered, but neither outboard engine would start. The problem was suspected to have been frozen gas lines.

Both of *Mesquite*'s main engines were shut down at 0312 hours. The Engineering Officer stated that "the main engines

27

were secured to prevent them from any damage, such as crank-shaft distorting, main generators from shorting out because of misalignment." The foundation for the starboard engine buckled from the lube oil strainers to the main sea chest. During the backing attempts it was noted that the flywheel on the starboard engine was wobbling "pretty good." The deck support just forward of the main sea chest had also buckled.

When the Engineering Officer learned that the *Mes 2* was not operating, he directed that *Mes 1* be lowered. The bosun mate who received the order remembered that the Engineering Officer was "very nervous and excited" and kept saying "we have to get a boat in the water." While preparing the boat at the rail, it was found that the raw water intake was frozen. While the problem was corrected quickly, it was made more difficult by the small boat periodically slamming into the steel hull, the result of the *Mesquite*'s rocking on the shoal.

Before *Mes 1* was lowered, the Engineering Officer placed his Bible and cigars into it. All the while, he was telling the crew

The passing merchant ship *Mangal Desai* assisted in transporting the crew of the *Mesquite* to Duluth.

to "please hurry." At 0354 hours *Mes 1* pulled away. A short time later she took *Mes 2* in tow and both boats stood off the port side awaiting instructions.

The *Mesquite* was informed by Station Duluth at 0353 hours that the cutter *Katmai Bay* would reach her by midnight (in 20 hours). Minutes later *Mesquite* told Duluth that the first deck was flooded from frames 74 to 92. The berthing area was buckling and compartments were sealed.

The *Mesquite* called a nearby Duluth-bound freighter, the M/V *Mangal Desai*, after noticing her on radar. Describing her condition, the *Mesquite* requested that the freighter proceed to her position and stand by. The freighter was expected to reach the cutter in 40 minutes.

The M/V *Mangal Desai* is a 606.9-foot, 17,822-gross-ton freighter registered in Bombay, India. She was built in 1983. The freighter was sailing under the direction of two Great Lakes pilots, Paul Halvorson and trainee pilot Randy Hayes, so she was well familiar with Coast Guard procedures.

At 0355 hours the Engineering Officer came to the bridge and recommended that they abandon ship. His recommendation was "desperate and almost pleading," according to the Commanding Officer. While surprised by the Engineering Officer's evaluation, the Commanding Officer thought that the damage must have been worse than had been reported.

At 0401 hours the Commanding Officer ordered the crew to prepare to abandon ship. Minutes later he reinforced the order to the crew, to be prepared to abandon, but not to abandon yet. He had just observed the Engineering Officer in his Gumby suit pacing back and forth on the fantail. The Commanding Officer commented to one of his officers, "Look, the EO is out there alone on the fantail with his survival suit on. He's no good to me now."

The Commanding Officer directed the Navigating Officer to do another survey of the *Mesquite*. A short while later the officer reported back that, among other items, the main hold had three inches of water on deck, dry stores had 18 inches on the deck and it was flooding at the rate of two gallons per minute.

In addition, the reefer space, vegetable, dairy and meat boxes were flooded, as were the engine stores. Hull damage was visible between frames 77 and 89. But the Commanding Officer felt they could still save her.

When one of the crew reported to the Engineering Officer (standing on the fantail) that the damage in the motor room was not as severe as thought, he replied, "F--- it. Abandon ship. We are sinking."

In response to the call to prepare to abandon ship, the crew mustered on the fantail and donned survival suits. Because the suits were stiff with cold, the crew had to help each other into them. The Engineering Officer was soon lying down on the deck with an "anxiety attack." Lying next to him was a crew member with chest pains. The Engineering Officer was repeating comments like "we have to get off" and "we are all going to die if we don't get off." To keep the panic from spreading, he was moved away from the rest of the crew.

Between 0442 hours and 0448 hours, the Commanding Officer informed Commander Group Sault Ste. Marie of his status. Among other items, he stated, "At this point the way we are sitting on the shoal I don't think it is prudent to try to move off, quite honestly I don't think I could move off. . . I am a little concerned that the damage may in fact spread a little bit . . . My EO has panicked, basically, and he is really no good to me right now. . . It appears we are holding our own."

The phrase "We are holding our own" has special significance on the lakes. Ominously, these were also reputed to be the last words from the captain of the ill-fated *Edmund Fitzgerald* minutes before she plunged to the bottom of Lake Superior on November 10, 1975.

At about 0500 hours, the Commanding Officer spoke to the assembled crew. He told them of the *Mesquite*'s true condition, that the M/V *Mangal Desai* was en route and that he would not unnecessarily place their lives in danger. He ordered them to return to their General Quarters station. By 0505 hours the crew was back in place and working to save its ship. The Navigating Officer replaced the Engineering Officer in Damage Control

Central.

When water was found in the bow thruster space, a submersible pump was used to control it. Attempts were made to clear the dry stores room of four feet of water, but debris kept clogging the pump.

As the result of the constant pounding, the *Mesquite* continued to deteriorate. In the motor room a small split below the thrust bearing continued to grow and was soon joined by others. Water flooded into the compartment. Before an effective pump could be rigged, the vessel was abandoned.

When the crew members returned to the engine room from the fantail, they discovered that the engine foundation and sea chest had buckled further. By this time the *Mesquite* was pounding "real, real hard." The second longitudinal from the keel on the starboard side, where it was welded to frame 116, had started to cave in. The pounding was also causing the weld between the second and third longitudinals to split. Even as a crew member in the bilge was hammering wedges into the splits, they continued to widen. Initially the flow was estimated at 50 gallons per minute. But with every hit the cracks increased. The flooding rapidly reached an estimated 300 to 500 gallons per minute. Unable to stem the flood, the crew abandoned the bilge. Bilge pumps could not keep up. Soon the lower level of the engine room was under water. When the crew finally left the cutter, water was halfway up the main engines.

At 0557 hours the flooding in the engine room and main hold was out of control. All spaces between frames 74 and 92 below the main deck were flooding. It was out of control in the bow thruster space, main hold, engine room and motor room. The order was passed to abandon the vessel. The crew again assembled on the fantail and donned Gumby suits. After the Executive Officer took a muster, he reported to the Commanding Officer that all hands were present. They were ready to leave her!

The Engineering Officer was transferred to the M/V *Mangal Desai* using *Mes 1* at 0605 hours.

At 0612 hours the *Mesquite*'s four life rafts were launched. Two were tied off to each side of the buoy deck. A cargo net was lowered to provide access to the port side rafts. Since the starboard net was iced over and could not be deployed, a Jacob's ladder was substituted.

The *Mesquite*'s power was shut down at 0617 hours. The *Mesquite* was now a dark ship. All communications with Station Duluth and the M/V *Mangal Desai* were via portable VHF-FM radio.

A minute later the crew began to leave the ship. As they moved to the buoy deck another count was taken and they entered the life rafts. The two rafts along the starboard were in the lee or protected side. Since only a Jacob's ladder was available to reach the rafts, boarding was one person at a time. The clumsy Gumby suits made progress slow.

The two rafts along the port side were filled more quickly using the cargo net. Instead of having *Mes 1* tow the rafts to the *Mangal Desai*, the crew boarded the small boat from the rafts and was taken over in it. *Mes 1* attempted to load from the port side rafts, but the wind and confusion of seas on the weather side prevented it. In fact, the boat nearly capsized. The Commanding Officer, still aboard the vessel, saw the problem and pulled both rafts around the stern and into the lee on the starboard where the crew transfer was accomplished without incident.

The log stated that the crew had cleared the *Mesquite* by 0830 hours. The Commanding Officer was the last man off. By this time the cutter had settled on the bottom, down by the stern and listing to port. She continued to roll from side to side.

There were no fatalities among the 53 crew members. Three were injured and medivaced from the M/V *Mangal Desai* by a Coast Guard helicopter from Traverse City. All three were taken to the hospital at Hancock, Michigan. Other than the panic attack of the Engineering Officer, one crew member had a sprained ankle and another a broken elbow. The chest pains case turned out to be asthma which was treated aboard the freighter by the *Mesquite*'s medic.

Chapter 4

RECOLLECTIONS

A s mentioned previously, the investigations relied heavily on interviews with all aboard the *Mesquite*. Some of those interviews provided special insight into the accident.

"The Three-Foot Shoal was Pretty Obvious"

Ensign Subocz's statements proved especially insightful. "He (the Commanding Officer) went below then. . .I brought the speed up to 120 turns. . .I continued to monitor the danger range. . .when the first sound of the impact occurred. When I heard the noise I grabbed the throttle and backed down as hard as I could. General Quarters was set and the CO was on the bridge instantly. The Executive Officer arrived on the bridge and relieved me. I stepped on the bridge wing, still trying to figure out where we had hit. Looking off the starboard bow I could see the three-foot shoal which was pretty obvious."

"BOOM"

One of the members of the buoy handling watch on the bridge remembered, "My job was done, I was tired, asked if I could go below and did. No sooner had I sat down than — BOOM! I knew we hit something because of the way the ship shook. I ran up to the bridge right behind the captain. . .He asked what happened. The ship hit again. Captain said to sound General

Quarters. Someone beat me to it. The ship was pounding more and harder."

"A Cheer Went Up"

Concerning his actions when speaking to the crew on the fantail, Lieutenant Commander Lynch stated, "I had the crew gather around, and I could see the fear in several of their faces. I told them the damage was not that bad, and it was too soon to be abandoning ship. By this time the M/V *Mangal Desai* was only three to four miles away, so I pointed to it and assured the crew he would be standing by if and when we had to abandon ship. I assured everyone that I would not endanger their lives unnecessarily and directed them to go back to general quarters. A cheer went up and personnel began to get out of their survival suits and go below."

"Buoys and Sinkers Swinging Around on Deck"

One of the repair crew spoke of the difficulties in rigging the pumps. "It took an abnormally long amount of time to set up the pump with my partners. . .because of the buoys and sinkers swinging around on deck." While watching a leaking vent he commented, ". . .we had taken a very strong hit and I could hear the decks and framework flex and creak in the compartment just aft of me. I immediately. . .got out of the compartment and dogged down the scuttle."

"Get Out Of There Now"

Two of the deck crew were in the forward hold stowing their "mustangs" (foul weather suits) when the ship struck the shoal. "We both were just about done when we heard the initial noise. We looked at each other, and at that time we heard it again. We started for the door when we saw Petty Officer. . .who screamed 'get out of there now and dog that door.' "

When the time came to abandon ship they were again in the thick of the action. "I was the first one over on life raft number one. I then started helping everyone in, one at a time, while still holding onto the lines and ladder to keep the raft as close to the ship as possible. It seemed like an eternity for *Mes 1* to come and get us, the whole time hanging onto the ladder sitting outside the raft while the boat would roll to starboard, and I thought it was going to roll right on top of me, and that's when I was really scared and thought I was a goner."

"You Could Hear the Bottom Grinding Into Her"

One of the crew had vivid recollections of what occurred on the fantail. "I started helping other people get in their suits. After awhile someone told me to get my suit. At that time I looked around and all I saw was orange bodies. I grabbed a suit, sat down and started putting it on. Someone came over and helped me. They told us to move by our rafts which were still in their racks. All the time the ship was rocking and rolling, people were being tossed around and you could hear the bottom grinding into her. People were falling and sliding around on the deck. We were told not to enter the water, the captain was coming to talk to us. We were told to sit down. Later the captain came out to the starboard side of the fantail. He turned around and told us to listen up. At that time, we took a roll to the starboard side and I thought he was going over. A couple of us reached for him, but he caught himself. He then told us that the most important thing to him was his crew's safety. He thought we had done a good job. He said we were hard aground and the stern was in 17 feet of water. He would like us to give it another shot. At that time everyone cheered. He told us to leave our suits on the deck and go back to our stations."

"They All Seemed To Take Their Cue From the CO"

One of the ship's officers later remarked on the Commanding Officer's leadership. "Throughout the incidents preceding and following the grounding I observed the CO to be in full control of his mental faculties. I saw no indications that he was not in control, and his outer calmness contributed to my well-being and the well-being of the crew members around us. They all seemed to take their cue from the CO and draw upon the strength he was exhibiting."

"He Kept Us Together and Safe"

A quartermaster recalled the abandon-ship drill. "I gathered the logs, charts and files for the QM1 (who was below decks). Then I went to the fantail with the abandon ship kits, some binoculars and a second chart of the area. I got back to the fantail, and we were all helping each other get into our survival suits. It seemed like a drill or something. No one was really scared or excited at the time. Just calm. A good sight to see. Then Lt.j.g. Bills and DC1 Gray came back and said the CO wanted to talk to us. The CO came back and said that he did not think that it was time to go yet. We still can save her, maybe. He asked us to go back and try. He knew what it meant to ask us to do that. Everybody agreed. We knew he was only worried about his crew. If the time came to go he would say go and not think about anything but us. So we all went back. We tried to stop the flooding, but to no avail. Throughout the whole ordeal, the CO's confidence and calm really helped me, and I know it helped the rest of the crew. He kept us together and safe."

"I Would Be Proud To Serve Again"

A crew member felt strongly enough to say, ". . . I thought the crew performed in an outstanding manner. I would be proud to serve again with any one of them, especially Lieutenant Commander Lynch. Not only is he an excellent skipper, but one of the best individuals I've ever met anywhere."

"I Never Looked Back"

Another of the officers remembered the poignant moment of leaving the *Mesquite*. "I preceded the CO as the last person to depart *Mesquite*. I don't think I can explain the emotion that seethed within my soul, nor the arctic void that was my spine, as I watched my Commanding Officer and one of the finest men I know take that last step from the Jacob's ladder. I never looked back."

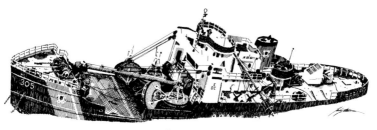

Chapter 5

INFORMAL BOARD ACTIONS

To help resolve the question of the possible impact of the lake's water current, at the request of the informal board, the Department of Naval Architecture at the University of Michigan performed a deep-water analysis of the wind-driven circulation of the Lake Superior basin. The analysis indicated the following information specific to Keeweenaw Bay at the time of grounding.

1. "The deep water wind-driven circulation of Keeweenaw Bay resulted in a clockwise gyre with a strong coastal jet (narrow high velocity flow) along the Keeweenaw Peninsula side of the bay flowing toward the northeast.

2. "The coastal jet flow increased in magnitude from near zero flow along the centerline of the bay to slightly over 1.0 knot in the shallow regions along the Keeweenaw Peninsula shoreline.

3. "Wind waves were also approaching the accident site from the south-southwest with wave heights from two to three feet.

"Based upon these predictions, the CGC *Mesquite* encountered a narrow current flowing toward the northeast which increased very rapidly in strength as the vessel approached shallow water. Simultaneously, the vessel encountered wind and waves on her port bow, with both contributing strongly to set the vessel in the same direction as the coastal jet flow."

A stability evaluation based on the grounding was conducted

at Coast Guard Headquarters on December 20, 1989. The study evaluated different scenarios of lightering the *Mesquite* and concluded that the vessel would "remain stable in the initial damage condition, with removal of all of the deck load, the anchors and chain, the sinker from the hold, the four NOAA buoys and all liquids." The effect of the lightering would have been the decrease of the mean draft by about one foot amidships.

The *Mesquite* had successfully completed refresher training in June 1988, with an overall excellent rating of 94.4. In recognition of its demonstrated high degree of proficiency and operational readiness, the vessel was authorized to display the Damage Control "DC," the Navigation "E," the Seamanship "E" and the Communications "E."

The informal report included numerous "opinions" reached by the investigating officer.

1. "That the CGC *Mesquite* finished decommissioning Keweenaw Point LB1 for the winter season and was proceeding to the next scheduled aid when the cutter grounded.

2. "That Ensign Subocz, while maintaining the Officer of the Deck and Conn, failed to obtain required navigational fixes in accordance with *Mesquite* Standing Orders or Coast Guard Regulations, and relied solely on a radar danger range from Keweenaw Point (one line of position) without due regard for wind draft, current or leeway before coming up to speed on the intended trackline. The cause of the grounding was personnel error, due to failure to follow established regulations, inexperience and naiveté with regard to the effects of wind and current on a vessel.

3. "That after, the cutter was backed away from Keweenaw Point to a range of 890 yards (after the buoy was on deck) and the cutter was then maneuvered into the wind (to bring the sinker on deck heading of approximately 190T) closing Keweenaw Point to a range of 640 yards at approximately 0130R. The cutter then drifted with the wind and current until at or about 0205R before the speed was set 60 turns (3.8 kts) on the intended trackline of 217T. Approximately three minutes before grounding (buoy deck lights were secured) the speed was in-

creased to 120 turns. Using the SAR Manual tables for determining leeway and wind drift, the cutter could have been set approximately 960 yards to the northeast and possibly more with the estimated one knot current. The Conning Officer was confident that she was in no danger because she had observed the danger range at 500 yards. Unfortunately, she was relying on only one LOP, there were no objects available for visual bearings and she was not cognizant of the set.

4. ''That Lieutenant Commander Lynch, the Commanding Officer, exercised poor judgement by not requiring the full Aids to Navigation Detail set on the bridge, considering the buoy was to be worked at night, in restricted waters and with the only available danger bearing extinguished.

5. ''That Lieutenant Commander Lynch exercised poor judgement in departing the bridge before the deck load and lights were secured, and in leaving an inexperienced OOD (fully qualified for only one week) without ascertaining the cutter's position with regard to Keweenaw Point, shoal water or the intended trackline.

6. ''That the *Mesquite* did not have a required lookout posted. A lookout may have observed breaking water over the three-foot shoal and warned the OOD. The breaking water was clearly visible from where the cutter grounded.

7. ''That there were no mechanical or engineering or electronic equipment casualties which contributed to the grounding.

8. ''That crew fatigue was not a factor in the grounding.

9. ''That the on-scene weather remained relatively constant throughout the night of 3-4 December 1989, and with the exception of its effect on wind current and leeway, did not contribute to the grounding.

10. ''That the damage control response of the entire crew was excellent, with the exception of Chief Warrant Officer Thanasiu (Engineer Officer and Damage Control Officer). This effort was in spite of the fact that the unit training had not been conducted in accordance with published standards.

11. ''That Chief Warrant Officer Thanasiu failed to properly man his General Quarters station by leaving Damage Control

Central in the Wardroom and personally inspecting damage, directing various activities (including lightering the cutter, launching small boats and making preparation for abandon ship) and visiting the bridge to make reports/recommendations. His failure to man his station and by directing other personnel (such as BMC Simmons, Repair Locker Leader, to off-load the deck and lower boats) contributed significantly to a breakdown in the Damage Control organization.

12. "That Lieutenant Commander Lynch and Chief Warrant Officer Thanasiu failed to systematically develop a plan for decreasing the cutter's draft by off-loading fresh water, anchors and chain, and the remaining deck load, which may have permitted the cutter to be maneuvered off the shoal.

13. "That with that damage recorded immediately after the grounding (basically the flooding of the reefer flats, magazine and dry stores), by lightering the cutter it may have been possible to maneuver off the shoal, preventing additional damage caused by the repeated pounding and eventual loss.

14. "That due to a personality disorder, which resulted in an anxiety attack caused by the stress of the grounding, Chief Warrant Officer Thanasiu lost control of his emotions, his ability to reason and failed to properly function as the Damage Control Officer. His actions were driven by his fear of the ship sinking should it be backed off the shoal.

15. "That damage control equipment was sufficient, available and, with minor exceptions, in proper working order.

16. "That the life rafts functioned properly and the only problem noted in the abandon ship evolutions was difficulty experienced by the crew in donning the survival suits."

Chapter 6

FORMAL BOARD ACTIONS

Τ he formal board reached numerous conclusions. Although some items that were not germane are not included, the most significant among them are:

1. "The proximate cause of the grounding of the USCGC *Mesquite* (WLB 305) was the failure of the Officer of the Deck and Commanding Officer to properly carry out and supervise the required standard practices of navigation in accordance with Coast Guard Regulations and the Commanding Officer's own standing orders while maneuvering at night and in unfamiliar, restricted waters. As the result of grounding, the *Mesquite* is lost.

2. "The following were contributing factors to the grounding:

a. "The Commanding Officer decided to work a particularly hazardous buoy at night.

b. "The Commanding Officer decided to work a particularly hazardous buoy without setting a full navigation team.

c. "The Commanding Officer decided to depart his bridge while in restricted waters without checking/determining the position of his vessel.

d. "The Commanding Officer failed to adjust his decision to work a particularly hazardous aid at night when he learned that the only available lighted aid was extinguished.

e. "The Commanding Officer and OOD failed to attempt to determine or take into account the existing wind and currents.

f. "The Commanding Officer and OOD failed to recognize the inherent danger of the 217-degree true departure course from the buoy.

g. "The OOD failed to verify the reasonableness of the danger range prepared by her watch.

h. "The Commanding Officer and OOD relied upon a single line of position (radar danger range) to estimate their ship's position.

i. "The OOD failed to ensure a fix was taken in accordance with the Commanding Officer's standing orders prior to making turns on a fixed course, after having been without a fix for at least 53 minutes in restricted waters.

j. "Bridge personnel had no clear-cut understanding of the shift in responsibility for fixing the vessel's position from the aid positioning team to the QMOW (Quartermaster of the Watch).

k. "The largest scale chart of the area contained a scale that is too small to allow a vessel to reasonably fix her position relative to the dangers present.

l. "There was no lookout.

m. "The bridge personnel failed to take, use and record depth soundings.

n. "There was no system built into the buoy positioning process that would ensure that the navigator checked positioning grids, danger bearings or tracks.

o. "The Commanding Officer and Officer of the Deck did not take advantage of the protective features of certain electronics equipment, specifically:

(1) "The Raytheon RANAV 759 Loran 'C' receiver that was aboard *Mesquite* has a mode called 'anchor watch' that provides range and bearing to predesignated positions thereby making the detection of set and drift readily available.

(2) "The Raytheon AN/SPS-64(V2) radar that was aboard *Mesquite* is equipped with a feature called 'autodrift' which provides a constant video display of range and bearing information to any acquired designated target, such as a point of land, thereby allowing for the establishment of set and drift, as well

as providing a constant estimated position. It also is equipped with a feature called 'true mark' which gives the user the ability to designate any position on the radar indicator display, even though it does not mark as a contact on the radar, such as an underwater shoal. This allows for a manually [cursor and variable range marker (vrm)] obtained estimated position.

(3) ''The Raytheon AN/SQN-15 fathometer which was aboard *Mesquite* has a feature that provides an audible alarm when the bottom shoals up to a preset depth.''

4. ''Crew fatigue was not a factor, but there may have been a general perception of pressure amongst the crew to accomplish the aids to navigation mission on Lake Superior in the most expeditious manner in order to return to their own area of operations.''

The formal board also provided some complicated calculations, hypothesizing how the *Mesquite* came to strike the shoal. In lay terms, the explanation as given by the Informal Board's opinion Number 3 seems the most understandable (see page 38).

6. ''The damage control knowledge and effort of the crew of CGC *Mesquite* were excellent overall (despite the terrifying circumstances), with the exception of the following:

a. ''The Engineering Officer wandered about the vessel directing individual actions which resulted in his failure to properly supervise Damage Control Central as it was his duty to do.

b. ''The Engineering Officer's failure to properly plot, analyze, communicate with and advise the Commanding Officer regarding an overall damage control or salvage plan negatively affected the overall damage control organization, effort and morale.

c. ''The failure of the Commanding Officer and Engineering Officer to develop a salvage plan, whether it be some combination of weight removal, backing off the shoal or flooding down to stabilize the vessel, hindered the damage control effort and aggravated the damage sustained by the vessel.

d. ''The pressure and stress of the grounding aggravated a previous medical condition (personality disorder), causing the Engineering Officer to lose emotional control with the resultant effect of his loss as a contributing member to the damage control effort and heightened crew anxiety. This longstanding condition may have rendered Chief Warrant Officer Thanasiu unfit for service on Coast Guard vessels.

e. "Despite the pressure and stress caused by the constant pounding of the ship on the bottom, the rapid progress of the damage and the confused sea around the vessel, most of the crew did an outstanding job of trying to save the ship. However, the performance of two individuals stands out. Damage Controlman First Class Gray and Boatswain's Mate First Class Signs performed admirably, demonstrating courage and leadership in the face of constant danger. Their professional response to this tragedy lessened the peril for others, inspired the crew and is worthy of further recognition."

7. "The damage control and survival equipment were adequate and functioned properly with the exception of the problems associated with the stiffness of the survival suits brought on by the cold weather and spray. The outboard motor for *Mes 2* failed to start due to frozen fuel.

9. "Had *Mesquite* been equipped with a side-scan sonar, the grounding might have been avoided."

The formal board made numerous recommendations. Among the most notable were the following:

1. "Lieutenant Commander John Richard Lynch USCG be addressed a letter of reprimand for his dereliction of duty and his negligence in the safe navigation of his vessel that resulted in the stranding and subsequent loss of his vessel.

2. "Ensign Susan L. Subocz USCG be addressed a letter of reprimand for her dereliction of duty and her failure to obey a lawful order as expressed in the Commanding Officer's Night Orders.

3. "CWO3 James M. Thanasiu USCG be addressed a letter of admonition for his dereliction of duty.

4. "Damage Controlman First Class Gene Gaylon Gray Jr. USCG be awarded the Coast Guard Commendation Medal for his outstanding performance of duty, as the repair party on-

scene leader, during general quarters set subsequent to the grounding of *Mesquite*.

5. "Boatswain's Mate First Class Ronald William Signs USCG be awarded the Coast Guard Achievement Medal for his superior performance of duty as coxswain of the Motor Cargo Boat during the abandon ship evolution of CGC *Mesquite*.

6. "The Chief, Office of Navigation Safety and Waterways Services, research the desirability of including in the Senior Officer Advanced Aids to Navigation course (ANC-OA), which is given to prospective buoy tender commanding officers, information covering the actions that are required, and those actions that should be considered, after stranding.

7. "The Chief, Office of Navigation Safety and Waterways Services, require the current edition of the Aids to Navigation Manual be amended to include a chapter on stranding similar to chapter 27-10-45 'Stranding' of the 1964 edition of CG 222, Aids to Navigation Manual.

8. "The Chief, Office of Navigation Safety and Waterways Services, review the various function modes of the electronics equipment aboard the buoy tender fleet to determine those modes that would be particularly useful in protecting the tenders during the time just before and after a tender works a buoy. They should include instructions on the operation and use of these modes in the Aids to Navigation School curriculum.

9. "The Office of Navigation Safety and Waterways Services review the features of the standard electronics equipment aboard Coast Guard buoy tenders to determine those features that are inherently useful to tender operations, such as 'autodrift' on the AN/SPS-64(V2) radar and 'anchor watch' on the RANAV 750 Loran receivers. That office should include instruction on the operation of these features in the Aids to Navigation School ANC-OA course, and as a lesson plan in the shipboard short range training program, and finally, as a Personnel Qualification Standard (PQS) for personnel who stand duty as under-way officer of the deck and as quartermaster of the watch."

11. "The Chief, Office of Navigation Safety and Waterways Services, require each district to review their floating aids to

determine which of those aids pose some particularly increased hazard (aids of particular hazard) to the servicing vessel and have that hazard prominently displayed in or on the aids record jacket in some color other than red.

12. "The Chief, Office of Navigation Safety and Waterways Services, recommend that each district review their buoys of particular hazard to determine if the danger posed by the aid warrants service by a vessel equipped with side-scanning sonar."

14. "The Chief, Office of Law Enforcement and Defense Operations, review the need for increased damage control training on our WLBs for our commanding officers and at least one other person in the engineering division in addition to the engineer officer.

15. "The Chief, Office of Personnel and Training, review the procedures for screening and assigning Commanding Officers, Executive Officers and Engineer Officers to afloat billets, specifically examining the need for medical personnel to review the medical records of personnel selected for assignment by boards and make recommendations concerning the physical and psychological fitness of those selected."

Chapter 7

CONVENING AUTHORITY ACTIONS

As Commander, United States Coast Guard Atlantic Region, which includes the Great Lakes, Admiral Howard B. Thorsen reviewed the formal board results and on June 26 issued his summary. Technically known as the "Action of the Convening Authority," Admiral Thorsen's document took an extremely severe evaluation of the investigation.

In part the report stated, "During the damage control evolution, certain *Mesquite* crew members performed admirably. These efforts were hampered by poor communications, an inadequate evaluation of the condition of the vessel and the lack of an adequate salvage plan. The crew merely responded to the flooding and casualties as they developed:

- "They did not establish and carry out a logical plan to lighter the vessel.
- "They did not consider counter-flooding to decrease the hull damage associated with the pounding of the hull on the rocks.
- "They did not take timely action to determine the depth of the water around the vessel.
- "When they finally lowered a small boat, almost one hour after the grounding, they did not use it to determine the extent of the shoal, the location of safe water or the feasibility of driving the ship from the shoal.
- "They never determined the danger of capsizing.
- "They did not attempt to pump out an aft fresh-water tank.

- "They did not drop the anchors and anchor chain to further reduce the weight forward.
- "Since the vessel was initially grounded amidships, these actions may have reduced the vessel's draft enough to remove her from the shoal before major damage occurred.
- "By dropping two buoy sinkers over the starboard (lee) side of the vessel, they created an additional hazard to the ship's hull while aground.

"The shortcomings in damage control efforts were caused primarily by the psychological breakdown of the Engineering Officer, Chief Warrant Officer Thanasiu, who did not perform his duties as Damage Control Assistant in a proper manner. Other key members of the crew abandoned their General Quarters stations to perform other duties. There is some evidence that equipment casualties, lack of adequate training and lack of adequate damage control references contributed to the damage control shortcomings.

"While there is no evidence that once *Mesquite* was aground she could have effectively removed herself from the shoal, the failure to develop a timely and adequate damage control or salvage plan insured the vessel's stranding.

"Beginning with the failure of the Commanding Officer to promulgate his own Standing Orders when he assumed command, through the failure to establish the ship's position for almost one hour while in dangerous waters and culminating in the failure to adequately respond to the grounding of the vessel, the Commanding Officer and various officers and crew of *Mesquite* demonstrated a generally cavalier attitude toward the principles of sound shipboard organization, prudent seamanship and damage control.

"On the night of the grounding, beginning with the decision to work an unfamiliar aid at night without a full navigation team on the bridge or any reliable navigation aids, the Commanding Officer and crew of *Mesquite* made decision after decision contrary to logic and sound principles of seamanship. At any time, a decision to exercise caution could have averted the disaster that befell *Mesquite*. These inattentions to duty built upon each other and together created a chain of events that caused the grounding of *Mesquite*."

Specific comments were made by Admiral Thorsen regarding the opinions expressed by the formal board.

"Opinion 4 states two separate opinions that have no relation to each other and need to be treated separately. The issue of whether any members of the crew felt pressure to expeditiously accomplish the aids to navigation mission on Lake Superior has nothing to do with crew fatigue. That portion of the Opinion relating to the pressure the crew felt has been restated as Opinion 10 below. Opinion 4 is approved to the extent it states that there is no indication that any member of *Mesquite* was physically fatigued to the point where it should have or did in fact affect his/her judgement.

"Opinion 6 is disapproved. Although certain *Mesquite* crew members performed their damage control efforts admirably, these efforts were hampered considerably by poor supervision, poor communications, poor overall evaluation of the condition of the vessel and a lack of an adequate salvage plan.

"Opinion 6e is approved. However, MK1 Huston should also be recognized for outstanding performance along with DC1 Gray and BM1 Signs.

"Opinion 7 is approved, but is incomplete. There is evidence that certain of the damage control equipment was properly set up, but never energized due to the shortcomings indicated in Opinion 6. Other installed equipment failed to work properly. Also, delays and problems associated with setting up the P-250 pumps is indicative of unfamiliarity with their operating control. Damage to certain of the other pumps and fittings may have been caused by rough handling during the incident, but such rough handling is indicative of panic or lack of proper training for such an emergency.

"Opinion 9 is disapproved. There is clear evidence that *Mesquite* did not properly utilize the electronic and visual aids which she had available. Although a properly utilized side-scanning sonar could be helpful to avoid groundings, there is no evidence that the addition of another electronic instrument would have caused the *Mesquite*'s crew to exercise prudent seamanship or would have prevented this incident."

Among others, the following opinion was added:

12. "Backing in an attempt to free the vessel after it was hard aground was imprudent and could have substantially increased the structural damage to the vessel. When a vessel is driven aground, a damage assessment must be conducted, soundings must be taken and a salvage plan must be formulated before attempting to back off with a full throttle."

The following actions were taken regarding the Formal Reports' recommendations:

"Recommendation 1 is disapproved. Charges alleging that Lieutenant Commander Lynch negligently hazarded *Mesquite* and was derelict in his duties have been preferred and have been referred to an Article 32 Investigation.

"Recommendations 2 and 3 are disapproved. Ensign Subocz and Chief Warrant Officer Thanasiu have been taken to Flag mast by the Commander, Ninth Coast Guard District."

Five additional Recommendations were added to the report.

19. "That Chief, Office of Engineering and Development, provide 180-foot class cutters with current stability and trim booklets with liquid load diagrams with clearly illustrated examples of their use.

20. "That Chief, Office of Engineering and Development, require the development of a Main Space Dewatering Doctrine similar to the current requirement for a Main Space Fire Doctrine.

21. "PCO/XO, MK and Engineering Officer schools should include damage stability topics in their training curriculums. Counter-flooding as a valid salvage technique should be included.

22. "This report and its results should be widely publicized to all Coast Guard units for its 'Lessons Learned' impact.

23. "The Chief, Office of Engineering and Development, should initiate a research and development effort to provide our vessels with microcomputer damage stability aids. Every compartment's parameters and description of damage could be used with liquid load calculations to allow for rapid stability determinations even in times of distress."

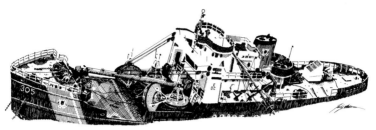

Chapter 8

IMMEDIATE SALVAGE EFFORTS

The Coast Guard reacted quickly to try to save their stranded cutter. Within four hours of running aground, arrangements were being made to charter commercial tugs and barges to assist in salvage. Early on the morning of December 4, a representative of the Coast Guard Maintenance and Logistic Command, Atlantic, was en route to the Keweenaw.

A salvage master, provided by the Navy Supervisor of Salvage, agreed to conduct the salvage on a reimbursable basis. Divers and other personnel from Donjon Marine Inc. accompanied him. Donjon is a well-respected and experienced commercial salvage company from the East Coast. The divers were in the water on December 4, 1989, to initiate a damage survey. The following day a salvage plan of action was completed.

There were numerous immediate problems with trying to put any plan into action. The site was extremely isolated. Local resources were almost nonexistent. While the *Mesquite* was a bare half-mile off shore, for practical purposes there were no roads that approached the beach opposite the vessel. Good harbors were not close by. What little commercial salvage equipment was left on the Great Lakes was in winter lay-up. Several days passed before barges could reach the scene. They were needed to off-load fuel and other equipment and provide a working platform.

The potential environmental hazard from spilled fuel presented a critical problem. Oil booms were deployed around the *Mesquite* as a safety measure. Approximately 19,000 gallons were eventually pumped out. Wisely, the salvors realized it was easier to contain a spill, rather than try to clean it up afterwards.

When they learned of the *Mesquite*'s predicament, the crew of the Canadian Coast Guard Cutter *Samuel Risley* at Thunder Bay "unstruck" and went to her aid. Eventually the cutters *Acacia, Katmai Bay* and *Mobile Bay* assisted in the initial salvage efforts.

The key to a successful *Mesquite* salvage, as in any salvage, was the weather. An estimated 10 days of calm seas were needed to patch the hull and haul her free. It was not to be. A storm on December 8, 9 and 10, accompanied by high winds and 10-foot seas, damaged her so extensively that further attempts that winter were hopeless. The blow had cracked additional hull plates, bent frames, toppled her mast and knocked the rudder off.

A special security zone was established around the vessel. Helicopters as well as Coast Guard crews on snowmobiles patrolled to keep scavengers away. During the winter curious civilians snowmobiled to the beach opposite to see the *Mesquite* in the ice king's grasp.

The salvagers, perhaps unfamiliar with the ferocity of Lake Superior's winter storms, originally thought they could just leave the *Mesquite* until spring. Then they could return and recover her. How wrong they were!

On February 1, 1990, the Coast Guard officially decommissioned the *Mesquite*. The decommissioning was an administrative move to allow the reassignment of the crew and reallocation of other vessels to return to their duties. As far as recovering the vessel to return to her Coast Guard duties, she was written off as a constructive loss. The question, however, of what would happen to her in the spring remained.

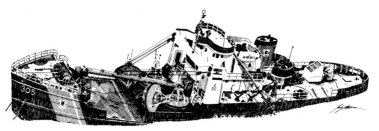

Chapter 9

DIVING OPPORTUNITY AND SALVAGE

Others besides the Coast Guard were thinking about the *Mesquite*. The Lake Superior diving community was vitally interested in the fate of the vessel. Two groups, the Alger Underwater Preserve Committee of Munising and the Keweenaw Underwater Preserve Committee, requested that the cutter be hauled off the reef and sunk as a diving attraction. The Keweenaw group wanted it sunk essentially where it was, while the Alger group would have it brought to the Munising area. However, the Alger group realized that their desires were secondary to the Keweenaw's. If it couldn't be sunk there, then bring it here. There never was any real competition between the two organizations. It was always apparent that the *Mesquite* belonged in the Keweenaw.

The Coast Guard had a different idea — haul her off the reef and scrap her out as quickly as possible. Any possible reminder of the *Mesquite*'s error must be eliminated quickly.

Some members of the Coast Guard disagreed with the official stance. One was quoted as saying, ''I would much prefer that she be buried at sea than brought back for scrap. To turn her into razor blades would be a crime.''

Scrapping the vessel would have cost an estimated $1.5 million; replacing it $35 million or more. The scrap value was only $500,000. Construction cost in 1942 was roughly $894,000.

The diving community found a strong ally in Congressman Bob Davis, the representative whose district includes Michigan's Upper Peninsula. Davis promised, "We'll put a full-court press on for that. I know it's been done before in Florida."

But to sink the vessel would require transfer of ownership to the state of Michigan so it could be used in the proposed underwater preserve. Given the Michigan Department of Natural Resources' long-standing policy of adamantly opposing any such innovative ideas, acceptance by the state would require a "full-court press" not only by Davis, but by all interested parties.

The Keweenaw Underwater Preserve Committee was strongly advocating including the *Mesquite* in the proposed Keweenaw Preserve. The committee was composed of representatives from the Keweenaw Chamber of Commerce, Keweenaw Tourism Council, Michigan Sea Grant Program, Michigan State University Cooperative Extension Service, Houghton County and Keweenaw County historical societies, tourism facilities, dive services and area divers.

Although in mid-1991, the preserve had not yet been officially designated, it is planned to cover approximately 103 square miles along the north shore of the peninsula, running from just

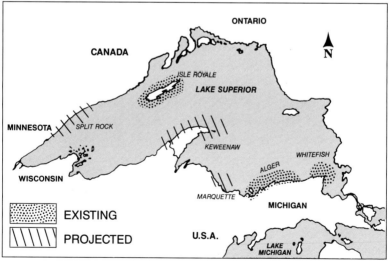

Existing and projected underwater preserves of Lake Superior.

south of the Portage Canal's Upper Entry around to Bete Gris Bay. The preserve would be about 65 miles in length and, in most areas, less than one mile in width. While Keweenaw and Houghton counties are included, 70 percent is in Keweenaw County. An estimated 29 wrecks are within the proposed preserve.

Other state preserves include Alger, 113 square miles along the Lake Superior coast near Munising and the Pictured Rocks; Whitefish Point, 376 square miles in eastern Lake Superior; Straits of Mackinac, 148 square miles connecting lakes Huron and Michigan; Thunder Bay, 288 square miles in northern Lake Huron near Alpena; Thumb Area, 276 square miles off Huron County in Lake Huron; Sanilac Shores, 163 square miles in Lake Huron; and Manitou Passage, 282 square miles between North and South Manitou Islands in Lake Michigan. Besides the Keweenaw Preserve, another new preserve off Marquette on Lake Superior is also expected to be officially designated soon.

Underwater preserves are not finance intensive. Little or no investment, development or refurbishing funding is required. A preserve is similar to a wilderness designated area. The economic return, however, can be significant. Some experts suggest an annual $2 to $3 million local impact from the Keweenaw Preserve.

Others opposed the entire concept of sinking the *Mesquite*. The Keweenaw Bay Indian Community didn't want the vessel sunk, fearing it would impact commercial fishing.

Also considered was the idea of moving her to a port to be made into a museum. But the extensive damage to the vessel over the winter — more than 80 hull perforations as estimated by the Navy — precluded this as a realistic alternative.

One factor that was important to the decision to sink the *Mesquite* was cost. To cut it up and haul it away as scrap was more expensive than the cost of preparing her for sinking into the preserve.

All items of value were to be recovered by the Coast Guard, whether the vessel was to be scrapped or sunk. However, her two Cooper Bessemer engines with their 1,700 KW Westinghouse generators were original 1943 equipment and were to be left. Their only value was as scrap since the *Mesquite* was scheduled to be repowered during the 1990-91 winter layup.

Sinking decommissioned vessels as dive sites and underwater habitats is not a new idea. Florida has intentionally sunk more than 30 vessels in its coastal waters. In 1987 the Coast Guard provided two former cutters, the *Duane* and *Bibb*, as part of the program.

Sinking the *Mesquite* was a first for the Great Lakes, however. Never before had a vessel been sunk as part of an underwater preserve. It was made possible through a 1989 amendment to the Michigan Bottomland Preserve Act allowing the intentional sinking of one ship within each underwater preserve.

The *Mesquite* may have been the first vessel purposely sunk as a diving attraction in the Great Lakes proper, but only by an accident of geography. On September 21, 1985, a Canadian dive club, with the cooperation and support of business and government, scuttled the M/V *Wolfe Islander* in the upper reaches of the St. Lawrence River, just where it joins Lake Ontario. The 164-foot vessel had been used as a ferry boat on the St. Lawrence. Placed in 80 feet of water off Kingston, Ontario, the vessel has become a popular dive site.

In late-May 1990, the 250-ton, 132-foot Grand Banks fishing schooner *Caroline Rose* was sunk as a dive attraction. The vessel was placed in 55 feet of water just off Driftwood Cove, about one-half mile outside of the boundary of Canada's Fathom Five Underwater Park. This unique park is located in Lake Huron's Georgian Bay.

The *Caroline Rose* was built in 1940 by Smith and Lunenberg, Nova Scotia, the same firm that built the famous *Bluenose*. Later used as a cruise ship, she sank at her dock in Owen Sound and was abandoned.

The *Bluenose* was a big Canadian Grand Banks Schooner, a type of vessel designed specifically for fishing the shallow waters southeast of Newfoundland and Nova Scotia. The *Bluenose* was especially famous because she was one of the last of the working sailing fishing vessels and participated in a number of organized North Atlantic fishing races. Her usual adversary was the Gloucester (Massachusetts) boat *Gertrude L. Thebaud*, thus adding an international flavor to the races. It must be realized that these were actual commercial fishing schooners, crewed by workers and not simply rich men's toys as is the case today. The first such race was held in 1886 and the last in 1938. Among bluewater sailors, the *Bluenose* holds a very special place of honor. The old film "Captains Courageous" has outstanding scenes of these special craft in action.

In April 1990, U.S. Transportation Secretary Samuel Skinner told Congressman Davis that the *Mesquite* would be sunk in the preserve. Davis announced, "Making the *Mesquite* part of the preserve is a fitting memorial for a well-loved ship that served the Great Lakes with distinction." Incredibly, the Michigan Department of Natural Resources had agreed with the plan!

Originally the concept was to move the vessel eight miles west to Bete Gris Bay and sink her in 100 to 130 feet of water. Coordinating the operation were representatives of the U.S. Coast Guard, U.S. Army Corps of Engineers, U.S. Navy Salvage, Michigan Department of Natural Resources, Keweenaw Bay Indian

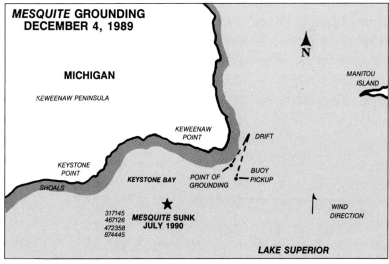

The *Mesquite* was moved from Keweenaw Point to Keystone Bay, where it was placed in 110 feet of water.

Community, Keweenaw Underwater Preserve Committee and Keweenaw Tourism Council. To accommodate environmental concerns that placing the vessel in the bay could damage commercial fishing, the location was later changed to Keystone Bay. Three Indian bands — the Keweenaw Bay tribe in Baraga, Michigan, and the Red Cliff and Bad River tribes of Wisconsin — had fishing rights in the area.

The actual salvage operation was conducted by Donjon Marine, reportedly the largest marine salvage contractor in the Western Hemisphere. Before the job was completed, it would test their skills fully.

To work the job, Donjon used the 180-foot crane barge *Weeks 297* and the tug *A.J. White*. Both were brought to the site from New Jersey, a trip of more than 1,000 miles taking two weeks.

Although the work was performed by the commercial outfit, a Navy salvage expert, Commander Bert Marsh, was on site and represented the Coast Guard's interests.

Before the salvagers started on the *Mesquite,* all sign of her Coast Guard affiliation was blacked out. A thick coat of black or gray paint obliterated all Coast Guard markings. This is normal procedure for any decommissioned vessel.

Accompanied by the hiss of acetylene torches, the salvagers burned away all of her structure above the main deck, including the funnel, pilot house and bridge wings. It was necessary to cut away the upper works to prevent any possible fouling of the *Weeks*' two massive cranes when the barge lifted the cutter. Removing the upper works also helped to lighten the ship, an important consideration for the lift.

The *Mesquite*'s rudder and mast were recovered from the shallows nearby. The propeller was removed by a diver for reuse on another 180. Working in the clear water of Lake Superior was a rare experience for the Donjon divers, more used to groping about in murky waters. When preparing to pull the wheel, a diver just tossed a wrench overboard. Jumping in, he swam over to it, picked it up and went to work. In the waters the divers were used to working in, he would have had to tie it to himself with a line to avoid losing it.

Weeks Barge 297 was positioned next to the *Mesquite* during the salvage operation in July 1990.

Workers had to remove materials from the vessel, lightening it to a weight that the barge could easily lift.

The salvage team confers with Coast Guard officials. The salvage operation lasted from late-June to mid-July 1990.

Salvage efforts included removal of potential pollutants and other materials from the topside deck house of the *Mesquite* prior to its removal from the vessel.

The superstructure and deck fittings of the *Mesquite* were removed before the final lift and move to the sinking site.

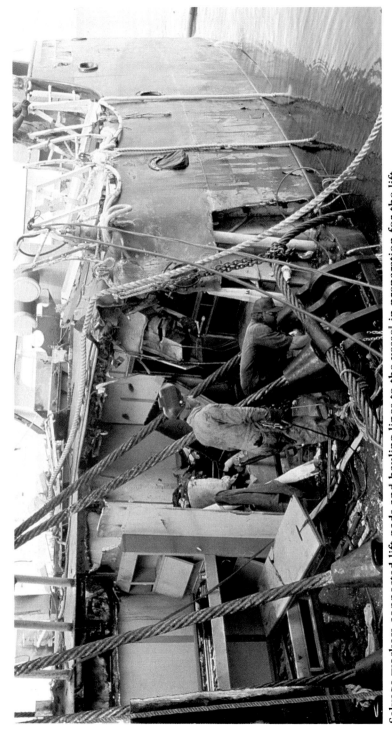

Salvage workers connected lift pads and hauling lines to the vessel in preparation for the lift.

A combination of compressed air and pumping was able to stabilize and right the vessel for the 1½-mile move to Keystone Bay.

Donjon Marine was responsible for the intricate salvage and move, which allowed the *Mesquite* a clearance of only two feet above the rocks of Keweenaw Point. With the added weight, the barge had only six inches of clearance.

Working conditions top side, while not dangerous, were difficult. The salvagers had to clear away much of the damage control equipment left by the *Mesquite*'s crew. Pumps, hoses and other gear were still in position from their aborted efforts to save their ship.

Donjon also stripped away all potential sources of contamination, including lead paint, petroleum products, batteries and so forth. To assure compliance, a representative from the Marine Safety Office inspected the work.

Even with the best salvage company in the world on the job, marine salvage is at best a very chancy affair. The variables of wind, sea, unknown structural damage, gear failure, human miscalculation — all can affect the outcome. But historically, weather has been the most critical. Just as a December storm prevented a quick recovery causing the cutter to ultimately be abandoned, so could another blow undo the best of the salvager's well laid plans.

The salvage plan was simple enough, although simplicity was not a guarantee of success. The *Weeks* was to be drawn tight to the starboard side of the *Mesquite*, and using the barge's two massive cranes, the cutter would be dead lifted until it cleared the bottom. The lift would be between 700 and 800 tons.

The shallow water made the lift difficult. The wreck was in only 12 feet of water. For the crane barge to handle the lift, it would need great displacement. In effect, as the *Weeks* picked up the weight of the *Mesquite*, it would be forced down. The trick was to make certain that it wasn't forced down deeper than the available water depth, otherwise it would ground too. According to the plan, when the *Weeks* took the strain she would draw about 10 feet, allowing sufficient clearance over the bottom to move the *Mesquite* off the reef. There were larger crane barges available, but their draft was too great for the *Mesquite* project.

In assessing their plan, the salvagers considered it possible for the *Mesquite* to break apart during the strain of the lift, even though two separate lifting points would be used. However, they thought that even if this unplanned event happened, the lifting points and cranes should be able to hold the cutter together.

The public was kept clear as the *Mesquite* was slowly lowered to its final resting place in Keystone Bay.

68

The *Mesquite*'s main deck as well as sides of the hull were still intact. Since it was the keel and bottom that were damaged, there should be enough strength left to keep her in one piece.

On July 14, 1990, the scheduled day of the lift, the weather was clear and lake flat calm. The salvage plan worked to perfection. The *Mesquite* was lifted the required two feet and carefully moved into Keystone Bay, about one mile distant. By 1915 hours she had been lowered 111 feet to the bottom. On the bottom, the cutter lists approximately 28 degrees to port. The highest point of the vessel is 82 feet below the surface. Her bow is toward shore, on a heading of roughly 310 degrees.

The operation, which began on June 30, 1990, took two weeks to complete. A summary salvage report was issued by the Commander, Naval Sea Systems Command in July 1991. It offered details of the shallow water salvage operation that might prove useful in future efforts. In conclusion, the report praised

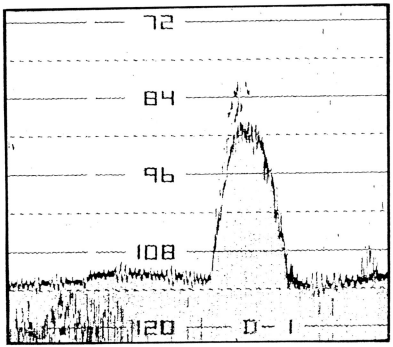

The underwater graph shows the shadow of the *Mesquite* sitting on the bottom at about 110 feet.

the support efforts of the Coast Guard in removing the wreck from tight quarters and relocating it in Keystone Bay. Of particular significance were the data gained in "the design of load-bearing systems, load monitoring, rigging and public relations."

In large measure, the *Mesquite* endeavor was predicated on the argument that the Great Lakes diving community had "grown up," that the prime motivation for diving was to observe the wreck and perhaps photograph it. But not to strip it of any artifacts.

Using the premise that items valued at less than $250 were not worth the administrative effort to recover, record and store for reissue, the Coast Guard left an incredible amount of material aboard the vessel. Items included silverware, plates, tools, office equipment, crew's clothing, pumps and machinery. The list is nearly endless. It is reasonable to say that most of what was aboard her when she hit was aboard when she was lowered to the bottom of Keystone Bay.

Unfortunately this is no longer the case. No sooner was the vessel down than bands of unscrupulous divers began to steal the public trust. Many of the items left aboard were soon being pilfered by the miscreants. As a result, local law enforcement agencies increased surveillance and the Department of Natural Resources began active patrolling.

It is hoped that once the area is officially designated as a preserve, the much stiffer penalties for such thievery will help discourage irresponsible divers from shopping at what has been called the *"Mesquite* Mall." Even now, penalties can range as high as a $5,000 fine and two years in jail.

There is no doubt that the *Mesquite* is a unique dive in the Great Lakes. Even with the bridge cut away, it presents a thrilling opportunity to explore underwater a vessel of a class that served the Great Lakes long and well. But there is real danger in the wreck and caution and common sense must be used. The vessel can be penetrated far and deep. Doors are not secured and overhanging obstructions are present. It is easy to become lost with deadly results. Caution must be uppermost in a diver's mind.

A diver inspects the *Mesquite*'s fittings at a depth of 110 feet.

Top: A diver investigates a port corridor near the *Mesquite*'s auxiliary generator room. *Bottom:* Files and equipment were left on the vessel in the ship's office.

The ship was sunk with clothes and personal effects remaining in the quarters.

Top: Diver Howard Durocher emerges from one of the stairwells. *Bottom:* Lake Superior's cold waters will preserve this poignant reminder of the vessel's last hours.

This illustration of the *Mesquite*'s final resting place was compiled from detailed accounts and sightings. The superstructure was removed and sunk separately.

Chapter 10

IMPACTS

The impact of the *Mesquite* loss went beyond the Keweenaw. It had a major economic and social effect on the Michigan cities of Grand Haven and Charlevoix.

Based on the assessment that there are more navigational aids to maintain in northern Lake Michigan than in Lake Superior as well as ice-breaking duties, and that the loss of the *Mesquite* left only four buoy tenders on the lakes, the Coast Guard reassigned the *Acacia* from Grand Haven to Charlevoix. Charlevoix had been the home port of the *Mesquite.*

As the result of the shift in stationing, the *Acacia* will now be responsible for 248 navigational aids. The vessel had been assigned to Grand Haven since 1979. Her previous home port was Sturgeon Bay, Wisconsin.

Acacia was the second to the last of the fleet of 39 180-footers built at Duluth. She was named after an earlier *Acacia* sunk in March 1942 off the British West Indies by a German U-boat. She has always been home ported on the Great Lakes.

Charlevoix had campaigned hard for a replacement vessel, and the decision to station the *Acacia* there was happily received. For Grand Haven, however, which calls itself "Coast Guard City, U.S.A.," it was a devastating blow. The Coast Guard decision was hard to rationalize regardless of the logistical facts. The Coast Guard had recently built a $2.3 million multi-mission station in Grand Haven, including Group offices and a search and rescue station. With the departure of the *Acacia*, it was the first time since 1931 that the city did not have a cutter. As the Coast Guard considers five buoy tenders an excess capacity for the number of aids to be maintained, it is virtually impossible for a replacement cutter to be provided.

In 1990, Grand Haven, Michigan, celebrated its status as Coast Guard City, U.S.A.

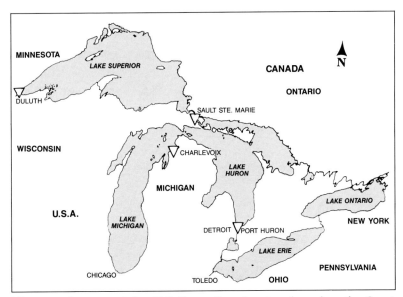

There are four remaining U.S. Coast Guard cutters based on the Great Lakes: the *Woodrush* (Sault Ste. Marie, Michigan); *Acacia* (Charlevoix, Michigan); *Bramble* (Port Huron, Michigan); and *Sundew* (Duluth, Minnesota).

The *Acacia*'s economic loss to Grand Haven was major. The crew and their dependents contributed more than $1 million each year to the city. The impact will be felt in retail sales, school enrollment and the tax rolls. The city considered the *Acacia* to be at least as important to the economy as tourism, especially considering the steady, year-round nature of the cutter's stationing.

Grand Haven's connection with the Coast Guard is strong, going back to 1877 and the first establishment of a Life Saving Station. The big cutter *Escanaba* was stationed there from 1931 until 1943. During convoy escort duty in the North Atlantic in June of that year it was sunk, either by striking a mine or torpedo. Within three minutes she broke in two, taking all but two of her 103 crew members down with her.

To honor the *Escanaba*, the city erected her old mast in a memorial park as a permanent tribute. The mast had been removed in 1942 when the cutter was converted into a warship at Manitowoc. It is reported that 20,000 people attended the unique ceremony. Within a year, Grand Haven raised $1.2 million in a community war bond drive to build the *Escanaba II*. This vessel is still in service and is home ported in Boston.

In addition, the city has what is reputed to be the world's largest musical fountain, also dedicated to the Coast Guard. The *Acacia* crew received several unusual benefits including having their YMCA dues paid by the city and being given free access to the country club golf course. For 52 years the city has hosted an annual Coast Guard festival drawing as many as 300,000 people. It is indeed sad that the Coast Guard cannot uphold its end of such very special community support.

The *Acacia* was moved from Grand Haven to Charlevoix, Michigan, in 1990, leaving Grand Haven without a Coast Guard mission for the first time since 1931.

Chapter 11

DISCIPLINARY ACTIONS AND HONORS

As the result of the investigation, the Coast Guard reprimanded both Ensign Subocz, the deck officer during the grounding, and Chief Warrant Officer James Thanasiu, the Engineering Officer. Ensign Subocz was fined $1,000 and a letter of reprimand was placed in her official file. She has been transferred to the West Coast. Chief Warrant Officer Thanasiu received a verbal reprimand. He has since retired from service.

While the actions against Ensign Subocz and Thanasiu were serious, they were nothing compared to what was in store for Lieutenant Commander Lynch.

Throughout the investigation, Lieutenant Commander Lynch took the blame for the accident, stating at one point, ''The deck officer made mistakes, but ultimately I consider myself responsible.''

After asking Lynch to resign, an action which he refused to take, the Coast Guard placed him under trial by military court martial. He was charged with negligently hazarding his vessel and dereliction of duty. If convicted by the five-judge panel, he could have faced dismissal, loss of pay and up to two years, three months confinement. The court martial was held at the Coast Guard Governor's Island base in New York.

Deliberating for eight hours, the panel found him guilty of hazarding his vessel, but innocent of dereliction of duty. His

Lt. Cmdr. J. Richard Lynch   Ensign Susan L. Subocz   Pilot Paul Halvorson

punishment was a "punitive letter of reprimand" and the loss of seniority of 150 in number. The latter punishment meant he was lowered on the promotion list, and he would lose revenue since he would not be promoted with his peer group. Lieutenant Commander Lynch is appealing this action.

The formal board recommended that Damage Controlman First Class Gene G. Gray Jr. be awarded the Coast Guard Commendation Medal for his outstanding personal leadership and professional competence during the grounding. The board also recommended that Boatswain Mate First Class Ronald W. Signs be awarded the Coast Guard Achievement Medal for his demonstration of the highest standards of seamanship and small boat handling while serving as the coxswain of the motor cargo boat.

One of the Great Lakes pilots aboard the *Mangal Desai*, Paul Halvorson, received the John T. Saunders Memorial Award for his skill in assisting the *Mesquite*. This prestigious award is given for special service to the maritime community. Commendations were also given to the Seaway Port Authority of Duluth, Great Lakes Tugs, North Star Marine, Guthrie-Hubner and the Upper Great Lakes Pilot Association for waiving the normal docking fees for the freighter when she arrived at Duluth in honor of her delivery of the Coast Guard crew.

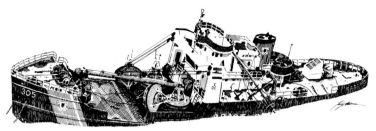

Chapter 12

VIEW FROM THE COMMAND

On April 25, 1991, the author interviewed Coast Guard Captain Jimmie H. Hobaugh on the subject of the *Mesquite*. Captain Hobaugh's experience on the Great Lakes dates from 1972 and includes assignments as Commander, Group Duluth; Commanding Officer *Woodrush*; and Chief of Readiness, Ninth Coast Guard District (Great Lakes). Before his retirement in June 1991, he wore three hats as Commander, Group Sault, Captain of the Port and Base Commander. Captain Hobaugh has more experience on the Great Lakes than any other officer on active duty today. As is evident from the interview, his opinions are both insightful and direct.

Stonehouse: Did having been the Commander of the *Woodrush* give you any special insights into the *Mesquite* grounding?

Hobaugh: Yes, I have worked that same buoy. I knew exactly where they were. I wasn't quite sure what had happened for the first few hours, but I know what it is like to get in that panic mode — when you are aground and pounding. But I never put one on the rocks.

Stonehouse: Did you ever put *Woodrush* aground?

Hobaugh: I used to put her aground all the time — that's the only way you can set some of the buoys that you work. Duluth Harbor, Keweenaw Waterway, Isle Royale. We never did that one very much — that's rock, but you pick a day to work some

Retired Coast Guard Captain Jimmie H. Hobaugh was Commanding Officer of the *Woodrush* when it was still based in Duluth, Minnesota. This photo was shot on March 29, 1976, during particularly tricky ice-breaking operations in the Duluth-Superior harbor.

buoys. *Harlem* Reef for one, *Cumberland* Point's another one. Matter of fact there are some buoys that you run the ship — get on the right bearing — and start the ship in through to set the buoy. If you work Sand Point Buoy in Munising there is the actual imprint of the bow of a 180 in the sand. When you go aground, you drop the buoy and you know it's on station. The same way with Keweenaw Lower Entry number four. You aim for a specific tree and when your jackstaff touches the tree you drop the buoy and it's on station. 180 sailors, as opposed to any others, deliberately, by virtue of their mission, have to work close to shoals because that's the job — place the buoy to mark the shoal or channel. So you are constantly working close to a rock or mud bank. It is not unusual for them to be close to the shoal, and you get used to doing that. It doesn't bother you.

Stonehouse: Was *Woodrush* identical to *Mesquite?*

Hobaugh: *Woodrush* was a C class. *Mesquite* was a B class. Between the two there wasn't much difference.

Stonehouse: Was Keweenaw Point Buoy an especially dangerous aid to work?

Hobaugh: I worked it day and night. I think I worked it six times and every other skipper has worked it the same way. It wasn't working the buoy that killed *Mesquite*. It was what happened after they worked it and backed away from the shoal. They made a mistake in navigation and judgement. The buoy operation went fine. They came up, picked up the buoy, backed away and secured it on deck. They were getting under way to go to Keweenaw Entry for the night and they just miscalculated, didn't navigate properly. They didn't really know where they were when they set the course.

Stonehouse: Of the Lake Superior buoys, which one do you think is the most dangerous to work?

Hobaugh: The one I used to hate the most was Point Abbaye. That's just down south of the Keweenaw Point buoy. The thing I worried about Point Abbaye, or any other buoy, was that you really didn't have good fixes — totally inadequate fixes. The skipper before me put her (*Woodrush*) aground on that shoal. That's all rock and it gets hard quick. Keweenaw Point never

85

bothered me. You could always back out. You had about 270 degrees that you could back right out and still be clear. Plus you could see that three-foot spot. It's basically the same with *Harlem* Reef over on Isle Royale. The water is much clearer over there, and you could see the shoal come up quick. But Point Abbaye just scared the hell out of me. It was rock. There were no good fixes and you really had to make sure that you had enough water. Keweenaw Point was just not a major problem.

Stonehouse: Any comments on the useful life left on the 180s? After all, they all were World War II boats. How long can they run?

Hobaugh: You have to understand how I look at ships. To me a ship can go on forever. You replace a plank or replace a keel piece, but the ship keeps going. I have been lucky enough to captain the oldest ships in the Coast Guard. I had the *Fir*, built in 1936. *Fir* is still going, and she could go forever. She was an old lighthouse tender, purely a buoy tender. Then I had *Taney*, which was built in 1937. She was part of an entire class of cruising cutters. Two of that class are still afloat as museum ships — one in Baltimore and one in Wilmington. With her old 400-pound steam boilers, she never missed a patrol — where the new ships of the Coast Guard — the pride of the Coast Guard — the bloody things were in the yard being fixed all of the time. Take *Bramble*. They picked her up in the yard and had to replace 200 square feet of her bottom and some rib structure. A ship can go forever. But the Coast Guard says a ship has normally outlived her usefulness after 30 years. The 180s are coming on 50 years. You can either build new ships or replace the bottoms of the old ones.

Metal on the Great Lakes — and this happens in the Great Lakes as opposed to anywhere else — metal gets brittle. If you look at the survey tapes (of *Mesquite*) you see the bottom was breaking up. This was not necessarily along the welds, but the plates were shattering, cracking all the way through.

Right up until that storm we were going to pull her off and fix her. She wasn't that badly damaged — until that storm. First thing we did was call the Navy Superintendent of Salvage. He brought his contractors. They did an interior and exterior hull survey and did a super job. Remember, at that point in time she was still sitting upright. We were going to do a quick patch job and pull her off and get some high-volume pumps. We could have pulled her off and salvaged her.

I have talked to some old buoy-tender skippers who were buddies of mine and some older than me. If I had been aboard that night and if I had the correct information, I would have backed her off and pulled around inside of Keweenaw Point and put her up in the mud. At least we would have been able to salvage it. The crew did a super job. They occupied their stations and had their pumps going. They were pumping her down. But the captain never found that out. The Engineer panicked. He was supposed to be in Damage Control Central where all of this information would be fed to him and then up to the bridge. He never got to DCC. The captain never knew until it was way late in the evolution (the true status of his vessel).

The son-of-a-bitch isn't going to sink. It's sitting on the rocks. Why abandon ship? But they did!

The other thing that happened on her is that, as she was pounding, the engine beds warped and froze the engines. But they still had the generators running which would have run the pumps.

When you put a ship aground you can do one of two things. You can sink it down so it doesn't move, or you can pump it out and float it off. Up until that storm, we were going to go down and patch from the inside or build coffer dams or use high-volume pumps to pull her off and get her into where they could patch her better and then take her to a shipyard. After that storm the bottom was just pounded completely out. There was just no way that we could pull it off and have it float. We would have had to pick it up and carry it somewhere. The nearest shipyard was Thunder Bay. The second closest would have been the Fraser yard in Superior. Getting her into either would have been very touchy. There was discussion about filling it with Styrofoam, but then it becomes a hazardous waste. So now you have a hazardous waste ship! Getting that stuff out of her would have been almost impossible.

Stonehouse: Was the *Mesquite* working under pressure to get home for the holidays?

Hobaugh: The Coast Guard put no pressure on anyone to do that. The crew might have been pressured amongst themselves to do that. I think they pushed it a little hard, but again the mission they were doing was not the cause of the ship going aground.

Stonehouse: The Coast Guard investigations spoke of the *Mesquite* not making use of the electronic navigation aids such as Loran and some of the special features of the radar. Can you comment on this?

Hobaugh: Let's start at the beginning. The OOD graduated from the academy that summer. She had been a qualified underway OOD for one week. She qualified in Lake Michigan. She probably signed off in Lake Superior, but she was not an experienced OOD.

There was a QM3 (on the bridge) — not your most experienced crew member. The Executive Officer was not on the bridge. The Operations Officer was not on deck. The Captain was not on the bridge. I would never, ever leave my bridge until I was at least two to three miles off of any shoal water and settled down on course. I would never work a buoy without the Operations Officer and probably the Exec. I might let the Exec sleep in, but the Operations Officer would be on deck. If I were going to work a buoy, I would have the full buoy crew, and the navigation crew would be there, too!

Their normal operations area was Lake Michigan. I don't know what the currents and wind conditions are down there, but there is a current in Lake Superior — and there is a current in that particular area. The water flow is up through Keweenaw Point and Gull Rock — and Manitou Island — that sets them, believe it or not, to the west. And that's what happened. They didn't have a good position from which to get under way and head for the Keweenaw Entry. They got set to the north and to the west, and if she had set her course from that position, which is what she did, it would have set her right on that shoal. She should have gone east and got a better position. I don't think they had a good position and that's what the investigation found. If they had got a Loran position and plotted it properly — if they had got a radar position and plotted it properly — they would have been all right. The positioning prior to getting under way heading for wherever they were going was just not accurate.

The OOD, the young woman, is one of the real tragedies of this thing — because she was a super smart young officer with a lot of potential. Still does, but I don't think she will stay in the Coast Guard. That would be an experience that would really sour her. I think we have lost a good officer.

Just because you are outstanding in an office, just because you have all of it in your mind, if you can't put it on the ends of your fingers, you might as well not have it if you are a ship's captain or a crew. You have to be able to take it out of your mind and put it on the ends of your fingers. Experience will teach you that. Proper qualifications — qualifications with people that are qualified to qualify you. I keep raising the question, ''Who qualifies the qualifiers?'' Before I commanded my first ship I had a lot of experience with a lot of very experienced people. Before they ever let me touch the ship, I had to prove certain things, and they stood over me and watched, correcting me. I feel that I was qualified by masters. I still have the question, ''Who qualifies the qualifiers?''

Stonehouse: During the interview you gave for the television program ''Superior Destiny,'' you spoke of trying to back the *Mesquite* off immediately. Realizing that the captain did not have a full picture of the damages, didn't he try to back her off without success?

Hobaugh: He never backed her full. He never backed full power. He never backed for more than 30 to 60 seconds. I would have put full backing power on her because every time the seas would raise her she would pound and hit. If she is lifting, she will come off. If you keep the power backing on her enough, she'll come off.

Here's something some of us older guys are asking. If you are trying to save your ship, to hell with the engines! If you can back her off and ruin the engines, at least you have a hull to put new engines into! I would have ruined the engines to save the ship. If you have two engines down there and one is vibrating — so it's vibrating — who cares?

Stonehouse: Do you feel enough effort was made to haul her off that winter?

Hobaugh: Yes, we had the tugs on site. We had the power to pull her off. But the object was to pull her off and not have her sink and become a hazard — a pollution incident — and to be able to make it a productive ship again.

Stonehouse: A security zone was established around the *Mesquite* for the winter. Were there any problems with vandalism?

Hobaugh: None that we saw. Before we secured her we stripped all the electronic gear and all the accessible parts from her. Then we locked her up. That particular winter we took videotapes every week from the air. They didn't go out there (to the ship) by snowmobile. If they did they were fools because the ice never made up hard around it. I can show you the tapes by the week where the ice was moving. It was a strange year. We didn't get the freeze-ups like we used to.

Stonehouse: Why was so much gear left on board?

Hobaugh: Let me tell you what the drill was on that. We got everything off of her that was on the topside decks. She was completely flooded inside — sewage tanks, lube oil and so forth. She was flooded right up to the port side overhead on the O1 Deck. She had dropped that much. She was so filled with slime and filth that at that point in time when we went out there to begin the operation, it would have been unsafe to put anyone down below. Number one, you couldn't get in there unless you were a diver. When you are looking at $25,000 to $40,000 a day for that barge to be on the scene without doing any work, you have to weigh what the costs are for that barge to be there with the people while you go aboard and take things out that are worth $2, $3, $10, $100 or $5,000. Then you have to look at getting the stuff out, clean it, restock it, reissue it, all of which takes money. What they came up with — they being the Maintenance, Logistics and Command representatives — was that it would cost us $250 per item to take it out. The paperwork, the files were ruined because they were wet. There was no sense in even recovering them. There were items left aboard that were ruined by virtue of their being submerged — pots and pans in the galley. They don't cost that much to replace. It's cheaper to put them down with the ship.

The other thing that we were told that we believed — that we still believe, and I think I made this statement on TV — she was built in Lake Superior; she was built with iron from Lake Superior; we took her home. We put her back where she originally came from. We put her in what we were told was a marine preserve — that she would not be stripped. We understood that it was not a preserve yet, but we thought and we believed in the basic honesty of the divers and the people that wanted her put there. We believed that she wouldn't be raped. I'm an idealist and a romanticist in a real world and on the real world side of it I know there are some unscrupulous #$%&*@s that will steal from anybody or anything. It's part of the world we live in. But the Coast Guard's intent was number one to save money, primarily to save taxpayer money, and number two, not to get anyone hurt. Throughout this entire evolution we have hurt no one outside of scrapes and scratches. If we had put someone down inside that ship and something would have happened — one crew member is not worth that entire ship.

The Coast Guard fights the budget battle every day. I could have taken my crew in there and turned them loose — we did take an awful lot of usable gear off her, but a lot of the gear that we left was either too cheap to take a chance with or was ruined. And there was a lot of gear we would have loved to have had.

Stonehouse: One of the recommendations from the official Coast Guard investigation was for an effort to develop an onboard microcomputer to assist with damage control and stability determinations. Do you have any comments on this application of technology?

Hobaugh: What you have now in ships of the Coast Guard is a Damage Control Central that has a series of charts showing piping systems, fire main systems and electrical systems. They have graphs and calculations that they make on flooding, counter-flooding — how much water you can put in one compartment to raise the stern so far and so forth. That is all done by hand. I have seen some remarkable things with a computer with a mouse. You can do that on ships and probably do it more rapidly than a guy writing everything by hand and making calculations by eye. You could do it all with a computer.

My problem is that I fly airplanes. I depend on instruments to do things. But what happens when they die? Technology is fine as long as you have an uninterrupted power supply. What happens when your power source blows diodes and all that stuff? All your calculations are gone! If you don't learn to do it by hand first, you are dead if that computer dies!

Stonehouse: To your observation, was there anything that made *Mesquite* special in terms of the ship or crew, anything that set her apart from the other 180s?

Hobaugh: I have a theory or a feeling about the personality of ships. To me they are a living thing. I have walked aboard ships and felt totally comfortable. And I have walked aboard ships and felt apprehensive. I have also walked aboard ships and there was just a blah feeling. *Mesquite* to me, and I never served aboard her, she was not an outstanding-feeling ship. But keep in mind I never served on her. I walked aboard *Woodrush* and I felt totally comfortable, the same for *Taney, Fir, Gentian, Iris* and *Unimak. Mesquite* had a reputation, no matter who the skipper was. You could put the best officer in the world in her or the worst and the reputation stayed the same. I felt she had an iffy reputation. It's a gut thing. There's nothing you can take to the bank.

Stonehouse: Any comments on Donjon Marine?

Hobaugh: They are professionals and they did a super job. They are probably one of the foremost salvage outfits in the world. Their competence is unquestionably the best I have run into. The capability they have, their desire to do it and their ability and their willingness to do anything to do the job was great. The people they had working for them are just outstanding.

When they say they are going to do something, they do it. They will figure a way to do it. They had some of the best people, from laborers right up through management — just outstanding. When you have the owner down there working like a common worker — that's a hell of a company!

Stonehouse: How would you rate the media's performance during the *Mesquite* incident?

Hobaugh: I think some of them wanted to sell news. I have a problem with some news people. They report things and don't tell the whole story. They write a lot of innuendos. I think if you tell the American people the God's honest truth — all of it — they will support you. The Coast Guard's in a business that we have to do that. We have to have the support of the people to do our job. The news media do not help us a hell of a lot. The news media on *Mesquite* itself did a pretty fair job. You will always have a couple of companies who will be sensational to sell newspapers — to stir things up.

Chapter 13

CONCLUSIONS

The wonder of it all is that the Coast Guard does not lose more vessels during normal operations. After all, implied in the mission of the service is to "go in harm's way," to sail in dangerous waters, perform rescue in the midst of storm and gale and to face the daily perils of the sea.

Even the lowly buoy tenders are charged to service aids to navigation placed in locations hazardous enough to warn other vessels away. It is the tender that must carefully approach and work them, then safely back off. It is a difficult, dangerous and demanding job. The fact that so few Coast Guard vessels are lost or damaged while going about their dangerous business is certainly a tribute to the remarkable seamanship of the officers and crews.

A troubling aspect of the *Mesquite* loss was the revelation during the investigation that the Coast Guard, as evidenced by the *Mesquite*'s operational techniques, does not routinely use the plethora of modern electronic aids to assist during their operations. The arguments concerning the use of Loran and radar positioning functions were eloquently made by the formal board recommendations. The comments concerning the use of side-scan sonar on tenders also deserve attention, especially considering this basic technology is 20 years old. Hull-mounted side-scan sonar would be of immense value to vessels tasked to service the buoys.

It is interesting to note that the mission of the humble buoy tender requires the most precise navigation on the water. Buoys must be placed in exactly the right location. Based on chain scope, a buoy can swing on a 50-yard arc, but the center point must be correct. Other craft depend for their safety on the buoy being accurately placed. While nothing can replace the basics of good seamanship and navigation, not to use the full spectrum of electronic aids is peculiar.

I do not suggest that the navigation of the vessel should rely solely on electronic aids. At sea nothing will replace the old standbys of compass, dividers, chart and experience coupled with good judgement. It is the former that supports the latter.

It is the person that makes the decisions. The technology is there to help, to provide the raw information to be processed by the brain. Over-reliance cannot be placed on any methods beyond experience and judgement. When the new technology goes "belly up" because of a power failure or surge, or simply ceases to function for whatever reason, it is the human, relying on the compass, chart, dividers and good judgement, who must navigate the vessel home.

A derivation of this line of reasoning is what is often called situational awareness — knowing precisely where you are at all times in relation to the objects around you. Whether in the open ocean or congested harbor, aboard ocean freighter or pleasure boat, the ship's "driver" must know where he or she is in relation to surrounding objects at all times. This includes hazards such as reefs. Good navigational techniques, to include modern electronic aids, can add immeasurably to situational awareness.

It is my opinion that regardless of any errors of the Officer of the Deck or Commanding Officer as delineated in the investigation opinions, had either the Loran range/bearing functions or radar autodrift/true mark functions been used, the bridge crew would have realized the danger and kept the *Mesquite* off the reef. This equipment was on the bridge of the vessel, in working order and fully available for use. That neither the standing orders of the *Mesquite* and Coast Guard procedure specifically requires their use, nor equipment operation is taught at any Coast Guard school, is absolutely baffling. If there is a true villain in the *Mesquite* incident, it is the Coast Guard itself for failing to utilize the capability of modern technology.

The argument of the Coast Guard for restationing *Acacia* from Grand Haven to Charlevoix was based on a better allocation of resources, in part that five tenders on the Great Lakes were too many in terms of the normal work load. Four were better suited from an economical management point of view.

This reasoning does have some flaws. That *Mesquite* was on Lake Superior at all was due to the *Sundew* being in dry dock and unavailable to perform her mission. While ideally such dry-docking can be scheduled for times when it would not impact on mission accomplishment, accidents happen, machinery fails and unscheduled work is necessary. Now that the Great Lakes tender fleet is reduced to four with the loss of the *Mesquite*, if any vessel is taken out of service for whatever reason, only three are left to pick up the additional missions.

If there was an impression that the *Mesquite* felt rushed and overworked trying to do her own mission plus the added ones as the result of *Sundew*'s dry-docking, isn't the situation far worse with only four tenders available? Hasn't the Coast Guard "economically" worked itself into such a position that the unscheduled lay-up of a tender will cause the others to either be dangerously overworked or provide critically less service? Where before there was a capacity for flex and surge, now there is a very brittle level of support.

REFERENCES

Alford, Terry. "Kingston's Newest Wreck Dive." *Diver Magazine,* March 1986.

Daily Mining Gazette (Houghton, Michigan). March 24, 1990.

Detroit Free Press. December 5, 6, 10, 12, 15, 17, 1989, January 10, 14, 21, May 4, 1990.

Flint Journal. January 7, February 4, 1990.

Halsey, John R. *Beneath the Inland Seas, Michigan's Underwater Archaeological Heritage.* Lansing, Michigan: Bureau of History, Michigan Department of State, 1990.

Inland Seas. Fall 1990.

Johnson, Dave. "The Final Hours of the *Mesquite." Nor'Easter,* January-February 1990.

Johnson, Robert Erwin. *Guardians of the Sea, The History of the United States Coast Guard 1915-Present.* Annapolis, Maryland: Naval Institute Press, 1987.

Kohl, Cris. *Dive Ontario.* Chatham, Ontario: Cris Kohl, 1990.

Lake Log Chips. December 26, 1989, January 22, June 25, July 9, 23, August 20, October 15, 1990.

Lake Superior Magazine. February-March, June-July, October-November 1990, December-January 1991.

Liberman, Cy and Pat. *Tall Ships 1986.* Wilmington, Delaware: The Middle Atlantic Press, 1986.

Mining Journal (Marquette, Michigan). December 5, 7, 8, 12, 13, 14, 19, 1989, January 7, 8, 11, 18, March 30, April 3, 18, 22, May 4, 5, June 14, 18, 24, July 1, 2, 14, 15, 17, 22, August 28, September 2, 7, November 25, December 2, 9, 1990.

Naval Sea Systems Command, "USCGC *Mesquite* Salvage Operation Dec. '89-July '90 Keweenaw Peninsula, Michigan." July 19, 1991.

O'Brien, T. Michael. *Guardians of the Eighth Sea, A History of the U.S. Coast Guard on the Great Lakes.* Cleveland: Ninth Coast Guard District, 1976.

Scheina, Robert L. *United States Coast Guard Cutters and Craft, 1946-1990*. Annapolis, Maryland: Naval Institute Press, 1990.

Scheina, Robert L. *United States Coast Guard Cutters and Craft of World War II*. Annapolis, Maryland: Naval Institute Press, 1982.

United States Coast Guard. "Investigation of the Grounding of the USCGC *Mesquite* (WLB-305) In the Area of Keweenaw Point, Lake Superior, 4 December 1989." January 8, 1990.

United States Coast Guard. "Investigation Into the Grounding and Subsequent Loss of the USCGC *Mesquite* (WLB-305) Off Keweenaw Point, Lake Superior on 4 December 1989."

United States Coast Guard. Letter Subject Investigation of Grounding of USCGC *Mesquite* (WLB-305) In The Area of Keweenaw Point, Lake Superior, 4 December 1989, dated January 8, 1990.

United States Coast Guard. "Investigation of the Grounding of the USCGC *Mesquite* (WLB-305) That Occurred at 47 23.8 N, 87 42.5 W On 4 December 1889, Action of the Convening Authority." June 26, 1990.

CREDITS

Richard Bibby — Page 84
Thom Holden — Pages 28, 82
Frank Jennings, USCG — Pages 2, 22, 59, 60, 61, 62, 63, 64, 65, 66
James E. Kliber — Cover and Page x
William Meierhoff Collection — Pages 4, 5, 6, 7, 8, 10
Wesley Mutch — Chapter Opens, Pages ix, 75, 97
Lewis J. Pavlovich — Pages 73, 74
William Reynolds — Page 74
Mark Rowe — Pages 71, 72
Paul Slattery — Page 18, 80
Tim Slattery — Pages 17
Eric Smith — Back Cover
Frederick Stonehouse — Pages 19, 20, 25
Ken Thro Collection — Pages 13, 14
Rod Thureen — Pages 68, 69
Steve Tiggemann, USCG — Page 27
U.S. Coast Guard — Page 12
Frida Waara — Pages 62, Back Cover

ABOUT THE AUTHOR

Frederick Stonehouse is a Great Lakes historian and author of 10 books on maritime history, including *The Wreck of the* Edmund Fitzgerald, *Lake Superior's Shipwreck Coast, Keweenaw Shipwrecks* and *Went Missing.* His articles have appeared in many periodicals. He authored the ''Historic Resources Study'' of the Pictured Rocks National Lakeshore for the U.S. National Park Service. He has directed a historic resource field study for Parks Canada and one on shipwrecks for Lake Superior's Isle Royale National Park. A frequent lecturer on diving, shipwreck exploration and maritime research, Fred holds a Master of Arts degree in American History from Northern Michigan University. As an avid scuba diver and underwater photographer, he served as a special consultant for the 1980 Cousteau Great Lakes expedition. He also participated in the 1989 *Edmund Fitzgerald* Great Lake Shipwreck Historical Society/National Geographic remote operated vehicle (ROV) survey and moderated the subsequent videotape review. He is a licensed Coast Guard vessel operator for all of the waters of the Great Lakes. Fred makes his home with his wife, Lois, and son, Brandon, in Flushing, Michigan.